Arthu

Morris

AN
ELEGANT GENIUS

Arthur Morris

AN ELEGANT GENIUS

JACK McHARG

an
ABC
BOOK

Published by ABC Books for the
AUSTRALIAN BROADCASTING CORPORATION
GPO Box 9994 Sydney NSW 2001

Copyright © Jack McHarg, 1995

First published March, 1995

ISBN 0 7333 0412 5

Edited by Evan Johnstone
Designed by Howard Binns-McDonald
Set in 10.5/15 pt Bembo
by Midland Typesetters, Maryborough Victoria
Printed and bound in Australia by
Australian Print Group, Maryborough, Victoria

3 2495

5 4 3 2 1

Foreword
by Jon Cleary

MY WIFE IS NOT A LOVER OF CRICKET. However, back in the summer of 1954–5, she allowed me to take her and the book she was currently reading to the SCG to see Australia play England. Her sole interest was to see Arthur Morris, whom we had met on a ship coming back from the 1953 tour.

England batted till 4.30 for, as I recall, 154 runs. My wife read 154 pages of John P Marquand, gone and now almost forgotten. Then Arthur came in at 4.50 and she closed the book but marking the page. At 4.52 Arthur was out for 12 to that journeyman trundler Trevor Bailey. My wife stood up, said, 'And that's it? Let's go,' and she has never been to a cricket match since.

It is a measure of her respect and affection for Arthur that she still considers him one of our dearest friends. When he and his wife Judith visit us, or we them, my wife may spend more time with Judith but that is only because out in the kitchen recipes are more important than batting averages and goulash tastier than googlies. She still thinks that the only thing more boring than the reminiscences of old men are the reminiscences of old sportsmen. The odd thing is that, knowing this, Arthur has as much affection for her as she for him.

As for myself, a cricket lover, I feel that Arthur has much to remember. Even a glance through Jack McHarg's book will show you what I mean. It was not the number of runs Arthur scored but the manner in which he did so. His footwork would be a lesson to many of today's batsmen struggling to come to terms with Warne and May; he was equally at ease against fast bowlers. There was a myth that Alec Bedser, one of the greatest of fast-mediums, had his measure and he did indeed take his wicket a number of times. Yet Bedser was also playing in those matches in which Arthur got some of his highest scores.

Arthur Morris will be remembered as one of the greatest and most polished of Australia's batsmen. He is also known, by those who have met him, as one whose intelligence and respect for the verities equal his talents as a cricketer. Not so long ago there were two gates leading on to English cricket fields, marked *Gentlemen* and *Players*. Arthur Morris could have walked through either gate and no one would have demurred. Not even my wife.

Contents

Introduction

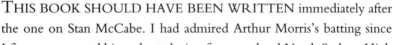

THIS BOOK SHOULD HAVE BEEN WRITTEN immediately after the one on Stan McCabe. I had admired Arthur Morris's batting since I first encountered him when playing for my school North Sydney High against Canterbury where Arthur saw out his school days. We later met in club cricket, I as an average member of Gordon's first eleven, Arthur as one of the luminaries of the talent studded St George outfit led by the one and only WJ (Tiger) O'Reilly.

Nearly fifty years later I asked Arthur to let me write something on him. He readily agreed and all was set to proceed when I was suddenly persuaded to do something on Bill O'Reilly, in 1988, a fairly lively 83. Bill had been a great help with *McCabe* and I felt we had achieved a certain rapport. Nothing about him had surfaced since his autobiography, *Tiger*, which appeared in 1985—an entertaining book but, like most autobiographies, one that skipped over some fairly interesting material.

With some diffidence I asked Arthur Morris if he'd mind deferring our projected opus for a year or two. Like the gentleman he is, he happily agreed.

So, at last, here it is, a tribute to a great player, fairly described by Frank Tyson as 'a cricket patrician'.

Of

Left-handers

Generally

'ANYONE, LIKE ME, WHO SAW HIM PLAY, still wonders about the relative lack of recognition and glory that history has accorded him.' The then Australian Prime Minister, Mr R J L Hawke, paid Arthur Morris this compliment in a letter read out at a dinner held in Sydney to mark the 50th anniversary of Morris's entry into first-class cricket in 1940. It was quite an entry: Morris scored centuries in each innings of a match against Queensland in Sydney, this being the first such performance in a first-class match on debut.

Frank Tyson, in a letter, dubbed Arthur 'one of cricket's patricians', which sums up his personal qualities with brevity and accuracy. And where does he rank among the great left-handed batsmen?

Writing on Frank Woolley many years ago, Neville Cardus said: 'No other living cricketer has moved cricket crowds to the happiness which has been felt whenever and wherever Woolley has batted.' Elsewhere he noted that 'there was all of summer in a stroke of Frank Woolley's.'

Among left-handed batsmen one would probably put Woolley near the top as a stroke player, although the claims of David Gower and Neil Harvey merit consideration. At the other end of the spectrum one might arguably place Bill Lawry, Ken 'Slasher' Mackay and Phil Mead.

Looking at averages, though, the positions would be reversed. Mead's first-class average is 47.67 and in Tests 49.37, Lawry's 50.9 and 47.15, and Woolley trails the field with 40.75 and 36.07. Lawry and Mead, for all their value, did not delight the eye nor move the heart. Woolley did both but was not wholly reliable—the nature of his cricket ruled out a high degree of reliability.

Between the two extremes there is a good number of left-handed batsmen who were both reliable and attractive. If they lacked Woolley's casual grace they certainly did not bore spectators witless like the other three mentioned. Among these Gary Sobers is pre-eminent—he was genuinely brilliant and his stroke play will live long in our memories. Then Arthur Morris and Neil Harvey could be bracketed. It is hard to separate these two. In comparing them one should remember that Morris throughout his career was called upon to open the innings for his country or state. Harvey usually batted at No 4 or No 5. Morris's career was fairly short and some of his best years were taken by the second World War. Harvey was a regular member of Australian sides from 1948 to early 1963 and gave wide-spread delight with his fluent strokeplay and marvellous fielding. Morris, at his best, was equally fluent as a strokeplayer. The averages of the two are fairly similar. Morris averaged 53.67 in first-class games and 46.49 in Tests; Harvey, 50.93 and 48.42.

In the next group of left-handers we could bracket Allan Border, Morris Leyland, Eddie Paynter and John Edrich. None of these possessed the qualities of elegance or brilliance or fluency of some previously mentioned, but all displayed in full measure qualities of concentration and courage and were sufficiently gifted as strokeplayers to maintain the interest of spectators. Leyland averaged 46.06 in Tests and 40.5 in all first-class games. Paynter's Test average is 59.23 (he played in only 20 Tests to Leyland's 41) and his first-class average 42.24.

And then there is the enigma of David Gower. Of all contemporary Test players he alone bears comparison in style with Woolley. An in-form Gower delights the eye—he makes batting appear the easiest of human activities. Sadly his form fluctuates so violently that, at times, his place in England's side has been in jeopardy. His averages of 44.25 (Tests) and 40.08 (first-class) put him a little below those previously listed. Perhaps, like Woolley, he is one whose batting average is an irrelevancy when put beside the pleasure he so often gives.

A notable absentee from those discussed is Graeme Pollock. He is missing only because political tensions have limited his Test match career. Those lucky enough to see him bat, and I number myself among those, would put him at the top. He had all the attributes of a player of the highest class—style, power, consistency, resolve.

More recently there is the West Indies prodigy, Brian Lara. His performances in Australia recently gave promise of great deeds in prospect. During the 1994 English summer, he scored prodigiously, breaking Bradman's 65-year-old record of 452 not out and recorded seven century innings in eight visits to the crease. (Bradman's was the first-class record until 1958–59 when (on matting) Hanif Mohammad scored 499. Bradman's was still the world record on a turf wicket.) Lara is an elegant player whose style is his own. As somebody said of Trumper, 'he has no particular style but he's all style'. However he has a long way to go before he takes his place beside Bradman who, after 20 years, at the age of 40, was scoring as heavily as he did in his youth.

It is axiomatic that an opening pair comprising a left-hander and a right-hander is greatly to be desired. Bowlers' lines of attack have to be varied as the batsmen change ends, fieldsmen have to be shuffled about—indeed the entire plan of attack has to be readjusted to maximise the effect of the new ball. It is not uncommon to see the line of bowlers, even those classed as 'great', disrupted by these variants, and frustration may creep in—with unhappy results for the fielding captain. Some degree of frustration extends down the line when left- and right-handers are mixed. Umpires, too, are not greatly impressed. The great Bill O'Reilly, the 'daddy of all leg-spinners' as Bradman called him, found left-handers less than congenial although he had a fair measure of success against them. Len Darling, an aggressive Victorian left-hander of the 30s, said he always found O'Reilly difficult. Bill's tactic was usually to blend in a more concentrated mixture of bosies with his other deliveries when bowling to Darling and other left-handers.

Morris opened the innings 37 times in Tests against England when Alec Bedser was the opening bowler. The 'Lion of Surrey' captured his wicket 18 times. In 48 first-class encounters Bedser had him 22 times. However, Morris's batting average overall against Bedser is 61.11— scarcely that of a 'bunny'. Bedser bowled predominantly inswingers to right-handers, or the ball that ran away from the left-hander, and Morris fell frequently to slips catches. This Bedser dominance, if such it was, did not extend to slow off-spinners. As the right-handers' off break spins away from a left-handed batsman, one would expect Morris to have been troubled by splendid operators such as Jim Laker and Hugh Tay-field. But Morris, in 1948, belted Laker out of the England side. Going down to Bristol to play Gloucester, the locals predicted that their long-serving off spinner, Tom Goddard, would cut the Australians back to size. In the event, Morris scored 102 before lunch with 17 boundaries. He was 231 at tea time and out for 290. Goddard was knocked out of the firing line with a damaged hand and lowered self-esteem.

Hugh Tayfield, of South Africa, claimed Morris three times in South Africa in 1949–50 and five times in Australia in 1952–53. Tayfield had a splendid series in Australia with 30 wickets at an average of 28, and was widely acclaimed as the finest off spinner to visit this country. However Morris rates him below Laker and considers his bowling tended to be mechanical at times.

Other spinners, either of the orthodox or wrist type, don't seem to have worried Morris unduly. Valentine and Ramadhin caused him some occasional anxiety but could not be said to have had his measure. Australian spinners of all types claimed his wicket at times but usually at some cost. Doug Wright, the English leg spinner, had him twice in Australia in 1950–51.

It is often said that Morris 'got it easy' in that he was not exposed to all out pace from both ends for much of his career as an opener. It's true that opposing sides of his day did not stack their sides with pace bowlers. This was an agreeable situation which reduced the danger of mortal injury to batsmen while giving spectators a measure of enjoy-ment, now denied them by boring fastish bowlers running from near the sightboard and banging in six balls per over short and lifting to the ribcage. But, scanning the pacemen Morris encountered during his short career, one comes across quite a few notable exponents. In Australia he batted against Miller, when the latter represented Victoria and took 24 from an over of bouncers. In South Africa he ran into Cuan McCarthy, a fiery and erratic exponent, and later Michael Melle, another genuine pace man. England produced Fred Trueman, Brian Statham and Frank Tyson, all more or less together. Only Morris and Harvey scored centuries against Tyson in Australia in 1954–55, although Tyson claimed Morris's wicket three times out of their seven encounters in Tests that season. Morris was a hooker of some note and one has the feeling that he might deal fairly harshly with some of today's devotees of the short-pitched ball. A reasonable reply to the criticism that he had it easy is surely that, while admitting Morris faced a less concentrated barrage of fast bowlers than batsmen of the present time, the latter have never been plagued by spin bowlers of the calibre of Wright, Laker, Ramadhin and Valentine, to say nothing of Clarrie Grimmett and O'Reilly. The shakiness of great West Indians like, Vivian Richards, Gordon Greenidge and Clive Lloyd when unexpectedly faced with the relatively modest talents of 'Dutchie' Holland a few years ago, suggests that these sorts of things even themselves out. Given the experience of batting against all types of bowlers, champion players would come through well enough in any era.

More than any player of his time, Morris shared the crease with Bradman. This would have to leave its mark, for the 'little bloke' was so much better than anyone else, as matchwinning batsman, tactician, analyst and what you will, that some of it would have to rub off on his partner if the latter were an average learner. As far back as 1950, Bradman wrote in his *Farewell to Cricket* that Morris was the finest Australian left-handed batsman since Clem Hill. Bradman quickly demolished supporters of Warren Bardsley by pointing out that it took Bardsley 49 innings against England to make three Test centuries. Morris, by 1950, had registered six centuries in seventeen innings. The Don might wish to modify his estimate of Morris in the light of the displays of some who've followed since 1950 but the only Australians capable of mounting a challenge would be Harvey and Border.

The latter, although a supremely good player who deserves our admiration and gratitude for his part in lifting Australian cricket out of its slump, and with a record in Tests that speaks for itself, is simply not in the same class as Morris. That leaves Harvey, and one would be inclined to leave that question open, although Arthur always considered Harvey a brilliant batsman.

Maurice Tate wrote in 1948, after watching Morris score 138 against Worcester in his first innings on English soil, that 'He is in the Clem Hill–Bardsley class', and thought the Worcester knock was the best he'd seen by an Australian left-hander on his first outing in England. He later added to his first assessment by saying 'Arthur Morris is streets ahead of Bardsley.' Bradman observed some technical defects in Morris's play but said that his ability was great enough to neutralise these, and added that he 'had a great capacity to absorb lessons'.

My own recollections of Morris go back to school days. He used to put his stamp on most games with either bat or ball. His slow left-hand 'Chinamen' deliveries à la Fleetwood–Smith were disconcerting to young players. Although he tossed down a few loose ones that asked to be hit, the whole thing smacked of voodooism to the adolescent minds of schoolboys. I remember his scoring heavily against us in at least one of the two school encounters in which I was engaged in 1936–37. Runs flowed in an elegant stream from a bat that seemed to be wider than the rules allow, and without edges. By this time he was a regular member of the St George first eleven.

Morris could scarcely have had two more competent mentors in his earlier cricket at district and state level. Bill O'Reilly at St George quickly concluded that Morris's left-hand, slow 'tweakers' were but a minor appendage to the spectacular promise of his batting, and soon had him opening for the club side. The bowling became an occasional relaxing variation to the main theme.

Playing with Stan McCabe in the New South Wales side before the war, Morris, like many others, fell under the spell of a batsman who displayed the qualities of the perfect cricketer. His effortless strokeplay, which seemed to have a slightly apologetic air about it, as though it hurt Stan more than the bowler as he inflicted punishment, reflected the man's nature—gentle, equable, without guile or malice. Morris made some of these qualities his own and was a widely admired and respected man, as well as becoming a player whose strokeplay at No 1 in the batting list, had not been approached since Trumper's day and certainly hasn't been since.

Early in the war when, after four years of sweat and endeavour, I'd achieved an insecure tenure of a batting spot in the Gordon first eleven, we journeyed to Hurstville to challenge the star-studded St George outfit. Led by the mighty 'Tiger' O'Reilly, the side boasted players like Morris, Ray Lindwall, Ron Moss, Bob Cristofani and Harold Stapleton. Moss later represented the State as did Cristofani. Lindwall needs no introduction and Harold Stapleton was an earlier edition of Alan Davidson. We had, on paper, a fair side—'Ginty' Lush and Bob Hynes were State representatives and Sid Carroll was later to be one. Sid was a player of the highest class who never caught the selectors' eye when Test teams were chosen. We scored 120, batting first, in a one-day match. My share was 20 odd—a freak catch terminated a not altogether convincing display. Fielding, we got rid of Moss cheaply only to see Morris and Stapleton systematically dismember our attack. I think Arthur scored about 80 and Stapleton over 100. Sid Carroll and I, fielding on the boundary, were tired and footsore by the time the clock had dawdled around to 6 pm. The one saving facet of the leather-hunt was that both the tormentors were left-handers. Lush had 1 for some, Hynes none for a lot, and the others provided batting practice.

Morris was a sportsman in the mould of McCabe and Hassett. He deplored the fashion (now generally accepted) of fast bowlers pitching short to tail-end batsmen and, as captain, directed his bowlers to eschew the practice. John Arlott, not one to dispense accolades to Australians on a lavish scale either in his broadcasts or writings, noted that Morris 'was one of the best-liked cricketers of all time—charming, philosophical and relaxed'. Stan McCabe would have been proud of the assessment and this view would have had, and still has, general support. He has a dry, some might say slightly macabre, sense of humour. Asked why he didn't take up bowls in his mature years he replied, 'I couldn't afford the wreaths.' He still enjoys warm friendships with many who were his opponents on the cricket field. The Bedser twins are close friends, and

Denis Compton, Godfrey Evans and the late Len Hutton were always on his visiting list on his visits to England. Among Australians of similar vintage, Keith Miller and Bill Brown rate highly and Sir Donald Bradman thinks the world of him.

He recalls that at the time of his entry into the New South Wales side, senior players frequently indulged themselves in 'taking the mickey' out of new chums. This did not worry Morris but may well have been upsetting to some others of sensitive disposition. Indeed Bill O'Reilly (not of a particularly sensitive nature himself), deplored the practice which led him to a less than flattering assessment of Bertie Oldfield. Bill said the practice ceased upon McCabe's assuming the New South Wales captaincy.

Alan Kippax once recounted to Arthur how he'd attended the opening of a bowling club in Bowral. The project had been promoted in its early stages by a German businessman who naturally enough was invited to 'say a few words' at the function. The audience consisted of a fair cross-section of the town and district, of both sexes. The German gentleman was lavish in his appreciation of the important part the ladies had played in the project but rather nullified the goodwill his compliments produced by saying in conclusion—'we must all tank de ladies and I ask you to give them de clap'. There were the sounds of muffled sneezes and coughs as the force of this observation sank into the minds of his listeners.

Morris toured England in 1948 and 1953, South Africa in 1948–49 and the West Indies in 1955. Like earlier visitors to the 'Union' as it was known in happier days, he rates the South African tour the most enjoyable of all. With Lindsay Hassett captain and E A (Chappie) Dwyer manager it could scarcely have failed to be a happy team, and the hospitality of the South Africans is well documented. The 1935 Australians under Victor Richardson and Harold Rowe felt the same. The England tours under Bradman and Hassett were enjoyable but games against England are more exacting than those played elsewhere. Bradman, particularly in 1948, was still haunted by the disgrace of Kennington Oval in 1938 when Australia suffered its worst defeat ever at England's hands. The Don, understandably in his final Test match season, was keen to expunge this disgrace and went about the whole tour with a determination both to hammer the Englishmen into the ground and to achieve a final triumphant 'first'—to go through a tour of England without being defeated. None of this is to say that this was an unhappy tour. Bradman was far closer to his younger charges than he'd been to those who'd accompanied him ten years previously, and the puckish Hassett handled the vice-captaincy with such ease and aplomb that any gap between the captain and the crew was comfortably bridged.

The Don, still very much cock of the batting walk in 1948, was appreciative of Morris's calm efficiency at the other end when they were batting together. The famous game at Leeds when the Australians snatched an incredible victory on the last day, found the two batting on a wicket that was tired and dishevelled. Grimmett and O'Reilly operating on it would have guaranteed early showers for all concerned. But England had no Grimmett or O'Reilly. Only Jim Laker in that side could be rated a top-class spinner, and in 1948 his skills were not fully developed. Laker took 3–113 in the first innings and 0–93 in the second. Norman Yardley the captain was reduced to calling on change bowlers Compton and Hutton. Indeed the latter was rarely deemed worthy of a spell in county cricket. Compton was a slightly different proposition. His left-hand 'Chinamen' of variable length but significant turn were mixed with an excellent bosie so good that some batsmen had difficulty 'picking' it. Arthur had worked Compton out in Australia in 1946–47. He was keenly aware that should Bradman be unlucky enough to lose his wicket early after the lunch break, it would be a significant success for England, and perhaps a decisive blow to Australia. He tried, as unobtrusively as possible but successfully, to face as much of Compton as he could. Jack Fingleton wrote in his book *Brightly Fades the Don* that Morris had enjoyed 'the choice offerings', adding 37 while Bradman made 3. This is a good example of how even the best of reporters can get it wrong when not in full possession of the facts.

It was indeed a pity that some of Arthur Morris's best years were taken by the war. That was a misfortune he shared with many. A sadder, more unusual event shortened his career at the other end. This was the premature, unexpected death of his first wife after a very brief life together. The knowledge that her life expectancy was short was a decisive factor in his premature retirement in 1955.

Between 1946 and 1955 he charmed crowds in every country he visited. More than that, his easy, relaxed personality and his perception of cricket as a game to be enjoyed, made him probably the best loved cricketer since Stan McCabe. This is entirely appropriate because Morris very early in his first class career, learnt correct cricket behaviour and much else from Stan. Those who have seen both players in their prime have a lot to be grateful for.

Early Days
of a Champion
and Then War

early difficulties, later triumphs

IN CRICKETING ABILITY, Arthur Morris and I are as far apart as the poles. I do share with him, however, one advantage or disadvantage depending on how you see it. We are both only children. It doesn't matter much now but the situation is a very significant one in childhood particularly, and indeed through adult life to some extent, while parents are still alive. Much is given, but there is nobody with whom to share the hopes and expectations. Moreover there is the risk of a surfeit of parental love which can become smothering.

Arthur was born on 19 January 1922 in the Sydney suburb of Bondi. He recalls little of his early childhood but it seems the Morris home was not a very happy one. Morris Senior was a schoolteacher— a rather exacting but fair man, with a deep love of cricket. In 1927 Mr Morris was offered a teaching post in Dungog, a town of about 2000 people some 239 kilometres north of Sydney and slightly inland. (The town's chief claim to fame is as the birthplace and nursery of Doug Walters.)

After five years in Dungog, Morris Senior was transferred again, this time to Toronto on Lake Macquarie and fairly close to Newcastle. There was plenty of sport, both in Dungog and Newcastle, and his father encouraged Arthur in every way possible. Cricket, rugby and tennis were readily available in the district and there was plenty of good fishing, particularly on the Williams River while at Dungog.

While at Dungog, too, Arthur first came to the Sydney Cricket Ground to see a first-class match. He learnt much from watching the great players who abounded in the thirties. New South Wales alone boasted Bradman (in the early part), McCabe, Kippax and O'Reilly and players like Ponsford, Grimmett, Woodfull and Richardson were regular visitors. Arthur recalls that his initial reaction to watching Bill O'Reilly bowl was one of annoyance because the 'Tiger' tended to cut scoring to a trickle and reduce the most brilliant strokemakers to plodders. Later in life when he played with Bill, he had an entirely different perspective on the great man's bowling.

During school holidays, Arthur would usually stay with his mother in Sydney; the rift between his parents at this time was widening. He remembers particularly watching Eastern Suburbs rugby league team during the winter school recesses and delighted in the wizardry of Dave Brown, whose scoring feats have never been approached.

At the age of 12 he was a member of Newcastle High School's first eleven, picked for his ability to bowl left arm slow 'Chinamen' which spun sharply from the off and cast a spell over young opposing batsmen. He batted last for the school. On Saturday afternoons he played with Blackwall's 'C' Grade side as a batsman and occasional bowler so that he was getting a good all-round knowledge of the game from both viewpoints.

Arthur had been travelling daily from Toronto to Newcastle by train to attend school. In 1935, Morris Senior moved to Newcastle to cut down on his son's travelling, but by 1936 he had obtained a posting to Dumbleton in Sydney, a suburb now known by the more fashionable name of Beverly Hills. Canterbury High School was the obvious place for the young man to go and he spent four years there from 1936 to 1939. Although his background and home life spent with a caring but undemonstrative father had inevitably caused some degree of shyness in his personality, the obvious sincerity and integrity of his character soon persuaded his teachers and contemporaries that into their midst had come a person of some quality as well as one of exceptional sporting ability. He walked into the school's first eleven, played Rugby in the winter, and was chosen for the Combined High Schools' cricket side for three successive seasons, and the Rugby side in 1938 and 1939.

At the age of 14 he was chosen as a bowler for St George's Shire team. One year later he was in the Club's second eleven as a batsman. At 16 he was in the Club's first eleven, batting in the middle order. His bowling was scarcely required by the St George side in 1938. With Lindwall, O'Reilly, Stapleton, Cristofani, Longbottom and Green, they had an embarrassment of bowling talent even when Bill O'Reilly was on State or international duties. O'Reilly, always a first-class judge of cricketers, soon concluded that Morris's potential as an opener was too plain to ignore. One Saturday afternoon, after winning the toss in a club game, Bill abruptly told Arthur to pad up as he wanted him to open. These were shock tactics, but Morris never looked back and rarely thereafter batted anywhere other than at No 1. In 1937–38, Arthur played in the A W Green Shield Competition, which is staged each summer holiday period and involves the district clubs but is limited to boys under the age of 16. His talents as a bowler were utilised in these games as were those of Ray Lindwall, and Morris still holds the bowling record for the competition—55 wickets at 5.23. It makes one wonder whether Arthur could have made it to international level as a bowler as well as a batsman.

His days at Canterbury were crowned in 1939 when he was appointed School Captain, an achievement he still regards with pride.

Arthur hardly ever got a bowl with St George firsts, but on one memorable afternoon he shared the attack with Bill O'Reilly and probably robbed him of a unique achievement. He took the opposition's last wicket after O'Reilly had removed the first nine. O'Reilly's feelings on this incident at the time are not known but, being the man he was, he probably had a good chuckle, particularly as Arthur's wicket was obtained from a full toss smashed straight at Ron Moss in the covers. Oddly enough, Ray Lindwall's progression was from batsman to bowler, while Arthur's was the reverse. Arthur Morris still considers Lindwall one of the leading all-rounders of his time. So strong was Australian batting from 1946 to 1953 that Lindwall had to be content with batting at No 7 or 8. With a Test batting average of 21, he was surely a very handy player at this place in the order.

Leaving school at the end of 1939, Arthur obtained a clerical position in the Prosecutions Branch at Sydney Town Hall and he remained there until he enlisted in 1941.

The Sheffield Shield competition was suspended due to the war in 1940 but some first-class games were played and Morris's club performances found him selected for four State games. In the first, against Queensland, he scored centuries in each innings (148 and 111)—a first for an Australian cricketer. Morris remembers the match very well and admits modestly that he had his fair share of luck in both innings. Doctor H V Evatt took him along to Stan McCabe's shop and invited Arthur to choose a bat with the Doc's compliments. He later played against South Australia where Clarrie Grimmett was still rolling them down, although close to the end of his career. Arthur found that Clarrie sent down straight balls for the most part but, after coaxing him to drive at first, he found he was being forced back more and more, and making errors. He was bowled by Grimmett for 33 and departed with an appreciation of the great bowler's patience and perseverance in achieving his victims' downfall.

While stationed in Australia he was selected to play Rugby for the Army and Combined Services. Some legendary figures, who were later to become household names in Australian Rugby football, joined Morris in these games. Vic Richards, Col Windon, Len Smith and Aub Hodgson are some that come to mind.

Coach for Combined Services, 'Johnny' Wallace, inside centre for the famous Waratah Rugby side said publicly in 1943 that Morris, in that year, was the best five-eighth in Australia. The Combined side defeated City Colts 57 to nil; Ray Stehr, rugby league international but playing for Services in this encounter, later remarked that they (City Colts) were lucky to get that, a conclusion of which Rex Mossop would be proud.

It is frequently argued that he might have gained representative honours in Rugby football and some New Zealand papers thought he might well be a candidate to represent Australia. Fortunately, the war brought an end to any ambitions he may have had in this direction and he never resumed playing after his discharge, a decision we may now gratefully agree with—for had he kept on with football, he would almost certainly have been lost to cricket. Ray Lindwall's experience was similar in Rugby League.

Arthur had taken up tennis in the early war years before enlisting and played regularly on Sunday mornings with St George Club colleagues Ray Lindwall, Bob Cristofani and Bill O'Reilly. The young men were encouraged by Bill's interest in them, and succeeded under the name of Eureka in winning a local B4 Division premiership.

Bob Cristofani at this time was a most promising legspin bowler who wreaked havoc among schoolboy cricketers while at Sydney High School. At a very early age he was well furnished with most of the equipment of a successful legspinner. From a longish run, Cristofani bowled legbreak, topspinner and bosie with good command of length, direction and change of pace. A useful middle order batsman as well, he was selected for the State in 1941–42 and performed impressively in Lindsay Hassett's Services side at the end of the war. His return to first-class cricket after the war was disappointing and, after losing his position in the State side, he played cricket in the Lancashire League but found that his future lay less in cricket than in business, where he enjoyed spectacular success. He rendered notable service as Australian Trade Commissioner in Ghana, London and elsewhere.

With five of his best cricketing years taken out by war, Arthur returned to the Town Hall for a time. His cricketing absences were considered to be excessive and he made the move to Stack & Company, a motor car distributor. There he remained for some years as a salesman with ample leave granted him to fulfil his cricketing commitments. Arthur speaks kindly of the management at Stack & Company, both for the consideration shown him in dovetailing his work and cricketing roles and, indeed, for their kindness to him at the time of his first wife's death.

Sadly, it is necessary to write something of Arthur's first wife and the tragedy which overtook the couple. He met Valerie Hudson in 1953 when she was appearing in the 'Crazy Gang' vaudeville show at the

Victoria Palace in London. She was a showgirl of striking looks and endearing personality. They married shortly afterwards but in 1955, upon his return from the West Indies, he was told that she had a life-threatening illness. Valerie never knew that her life expectancy was short but Arthur determined that he would get her home to England to see her family. The opportunity presented itself when the 1956 Australian tourists were chosen. With help from Valerie's old employer, a reporting contract with the London *Daily Express*, and Lindsay Hassett, Arthur was able to carry out his heart-wrenching plan. Valerie died shortly after her return to Australia, at the age of 33 and after only 18 months of marriage. This was a shattering experience.

Towards the end of the fifties he was persuaded by a cricketing friend J G (Ginty) Lush, to participate in the promotion of ten-pin bowling in Australia. 'Ginty' Lush had been a legendary figure at North Sydney High School and later a player of note for the Mosman and Gordon Clubs and the New South Wales State side. As an all-round cricketer, he was not far short of the highest class. An aggressive middle order batsman, a very fast, if somewhat erratic opening bowler, a splendid fieldsman anywhere and a captain who had the God-given gift of extracting the last ounce of loyalty from his subordinates, Ginty Lush was a man anybody would be proud to know. Handsome, outgoing and charming in manner, he had many of Stan McCabe's qualities, although he was rather more assertive than Stan. He had a successful career in journalism but, at this particular time in Arthur Morris's life, he was bent on kick-starting 'AMF' ten-pin bowling in his native land.

Arthur and Ginty went to the United States to get the basic data necessary to help launch the project in Australia. This was an interesting trip, enlivened by Ginty's occasional and unpredictable exuberance. On one occasion, the two entrepreneurs were resting from their labours in Washington DC by taking in a film at one of the city's theatres. The film happened to be *Ben Hur*. Towards the end, when the famous chariot race was nearing the finishing line, Lush, a keen follower of horse racing, stood up and shouted through cupped hands: 'Take the inside Ben! Take the inside!' Ben must have heard him and, following the advice given, romped in ahead of a star-studded field. Arthur Morris shrunk further down in his seat and waited in some trepidation for the film to end and the lights to come on. This happened very shortly after correct weight was declared and Morris got up to make as quick an exit as he could. Lush had skipped in the dark leaving an embarrassed Arthur Morris to wear the puzzled gaze of most of the audience. To round off this period in Arthur's business career, it may be said that ten-pin bowling was slow to take off in Australia, although now fairly popular, and the two promoters did not profit greatly from the enterprise.

Doug Insole, Essex and England player, persuaded Arthur to join George Wimpey and Company, a British-based building and engineering firm. After a period with them, he moved on to Wormald's Limited with whom he stayed until he retired in the late 1980s.

He married, in 1968, Judith Menmuir of Western Australia. Judith complements him perfectly, and is interested in and proud of his achievements. Arthur was a Trustee of the Sydney Cricket Ground for 22 years and for eight of these, Deputy Chairman. With Pat Hills, former Lord Mayor of Sydney and State Labor member of Parliament, and fellow Trustees, he was heavily involved in the modernising of the old ground which included the construction of the Don Bradman Stand, bordered on one side by the earlier MA Noble Stand and later, on the other side, by the Bill O'Reilly Stand. While these improvements were essential for the comfort and control of spectators, the Bradman Stand at the northern end has, unfortunately, blocked the cooling north easterly breeze which is so important a characteristic of a Sydney summer. Bill O'Reilly loved bowling from the Paddington end at Sydney with the nor'easter coming in behind him and over his left shoulder. One of O'Reilly's unique qualities as a spin bowler was his preference for bowling with the wind. When the southerly blew at Sydney, Bill switched to the Randwick end but was slightly less effective, probably because the southerly lacked the nor'easter's humidity factor.

Arthur was also a delegate from St George to the New South Wales Cricket Association and was a Vice President until problems arose with World Series Cricket in the late seventies. These involved Morris in a conflict of interest due to his position as a SCG Trustee—the Trust was then involved in a dispute with the Cricket Association over use of the ground by World Series Cricket.

Arthur and Judith lived in Sydney for some years after Arthur retired from Wormald's. He did some part time work for a while until family reasons suggested that a move to Cessnock was necessary, and the couple moved there in late 1989. Arthur still travels regularly to Sydney for meetings. He maintains contact with his cricketing friends and still, approaching 73 years of age, plays tennis in a very energetic fashion. When pressed he will acknowledge receipt of the MBE in 1974 'for services to sport.'

Morris's war service excluded him from the Australian side which toured New Zealand under Bill Brown's captaincy in early 1946. This tour, with its solitary Test, was the last in which Bill O'Reilly played. Arthur did not gain exalted rank in the Army and left it as he'd joined, a private. Eligibility for Lindsay Hassett's Services side towards the end of the European war was confined to members of the AIF who'd served in the Middle east, plus RAAF and RAN personnel who served overseas. Arthur's war service was confined to New Guinea (as was Ray Lindwall's) which ruled them out of consideration.

The aunt, his father's cousin, who had cared for the pair throughout their lives after the breakdown of Morris Senior's marriage, died in 1988 at the age of 96. It was a severe loss, although her direct involvement in his affairs had, of course, ceased years before. She had been, though, 'in loco parentis' and her death came as a shock. Arthur was about to board an aeroplane at Sydney to fly to Adelaide where he was listed to speak at the Australian Cricket Society's annual dinner. He was told of his aunt's death and promptly cancelled the flight and the speaking engagement. The latter commitment was taken over, at short notice and very ably, by Jack Potter who was at that time Director of the Cricket Academy in Adelaide. Morris is an effective speaker and delighted the guests at the Sydney dinner given in his honour in 1990, at which Prime Minister Hawke's letter was read to the gathering.

The Morrises are a long-lived family. Arthur's father died in 1984 at the age of 96, his mother in 1992 aged 90. Following the breakdown of their marriage, Mrs Morris Snr had married Don McQualter, Headmaster of Bondi Beach Public School. Arthur had a very happy relationship with Don who is still alive and well.

Arthur now lives quietly with Judith in Cessnock, about two hour's drive from the Sydney GPO, playing tennis regularly and making regular forays into the Hunter Valley to cast an experienced eye over the wines which are such a feature of that fertile district. He appears happy and relaxed.

He has various cricketing contacts in the United Kingdom and is fortunate in being able to renew these friendships from time to time. The Bedsers, Denis Compton, Peter May and Colin Cowdrey are just a few who welcome him on his visits and the old battles are fought again, time having added special lustre to them. Bill Brown, Lindsay Hassett, Neil Harvey, Bill O'Reilly, Keith Miller, Ian Johnson and that rare batting genius, Bill Johnston, all figured frequently in the Morris's lives until Bill and Lindsay died early in the 1990s. Cricket is like that.

One of Arthur's overseas friends is a wealthy member of Lord's Taverners in London, Rafael Djanogly. The pair met at the Centenary Test in London in 1980. Mr Djanogly later invited Arthur and Judith to Bill Edrich's 70th birthday party in London in 1986 and the friendship has blossomed latterly. Djanogly has provided accommodation for Arthur and Judith as well as assisting with such bothersome details as airfares on two further visits to London for Arthur and Judith.

On the first of these in 1988, Djanogly mentioned he had arranged a 'small dinner party' in Arthur's honour at Claridges. 'How many will be there?' enquired Morris. 'One hundred and forty six' replied Djanogly, 'including the Archbishop of Canterbury and his wife'. 'What about the Pope?' asked a thunderstruck Morris. 'He's in Africa and the Chief Rabbi can't make it' was the reply.

Included in the 'small' gathering were old friends Peter May, Freddie Brown, John Warr, Colin Cowdrey, Trevor Bailey, Len Hutton, leading cricket officials and members of the Lord's Taverners.

First Brush

with 'The Poms'

1946–47

two immortals—D G Bradman and A V Bedser

AT THE CONCLUSION OF HOSTILITIES IN HITLER'S WAR, Australian cricket administrators were keen that the Tests between England and Australia be resumed as quickly as possible. The MCC was not so enthusiastic, pointing out that England had suffered six years of conflict with food rationing severe and likely to remain so. They understandably felt that the dice was loaded a little heavily in Australia's favour. Hedley Verity and Kenneth Farnes had lost their lives in the struggle and, although both would have been past their cricketing prime, at least in Australian terms, they might well have provided some stiffening to what subsequently turned out to be a fairly mediocre bowling line-up.

However, recognising the need to get things moving again, and in response to Australian pressure, the MCC agreed to send a side here in the 1946–47 season. The formidable figure of Walter Hammond, now in his 44th year, stuck out a mile as the man most suitable to lead this revival. He had been in splendid form during the 'Victory Tests' and the years appeared to have dealt kindly with him. In the event Hammond proved to be something of a disappointment despite some fine batting, particularly on rain-affected wickets. He appeared baffled by Colin McCool's leg spin—those who'd seen him demolish Grimmett and Frank Ward before the war could not understand this. He never really seemed to come to grips with the captaincy side of his duties either on or off the field and, on the whole, it was a rather unhappy finale to a player who many considered ranked with Jack Hobbs as the finest English batsmen between the wars.

Arthur Morris once out of the army was quickly in form making a splendid 68 for St George in a club match against Marrickville, although he was rebuked by Bill O'Reilly for 'throwing his wicket away'. He followed with a brisk 111 not out for Jack Chegwyn's eleven against Maitland. Selection in the State side to play Queensland seemed to be a formality following a further century against Manly. Cricket scribes were talking about him as a potential Test all-rounder after he captured 6–47 in a club game. This viewpoint gained little support among the powers that be. Morris had a successful match in Brisbane with 27 and 98. Ginty Lush wrote that Morris's placement of the ball excelled even Bradman at his top, which is heady praise.

The MCC team was proceeding around the continent in its time-honoured anti-clockwise direction, and much interest and conjecture centred on the progress of Don Bradman. He was taking some tentative steps towards a come-back and after an outing against the Englishmen in Adelaide where he scored 76, Don agreed to lead the 'Australian XI' side in the Melbourne game played as a forerunner to the Tests. With Morris, Bradman added 196 for the second wicket. Arthur's innings of 115 occupied 297 minutes and was described as a 'typical Test opener's innings'. With only two boundaries it was rather out of character, but most effective in sealing a position in the Test team. Bradman scored 106 despite some physical discomfort.

Ray Robinson wrote that Morris's bat was 'all middle and no edges'. Bradman's century knock sufficed to persuade him that he was fit enough to play Test cricket, a decision no doubt received with very mixed feelings by the Englishmen.

In the rain-affected game against the tourists at Sydney, Morris was again in the runs with 81 not out in the total of 4–165. Sid Barnes, captain, batted at No 3 and was out for 1.

Morris's early season run of successes came to a sudden end in the

Brisbane and Sydney Tests where his contributions were 2 and 5 and he spent lengthy unproductive periods in the pavilion watching his team-mates pile on the runs. Bedser had him caught at slip by Hammond at Brisbane and at Sydney he dragged a ball from part-time bowler, Bill Edrich, onto his wicket.

After his first encounter with Alec Bedser, Arthur quickly grasped that in the big Englishman with the outsized hands, he'd met a bowler of skill and determination beside whom medium pacers like Maurice Sievers of Victoria and Geoff Cook of Queensland had nothing in common other than that all three bowled right hand. The copybook 'side on' action, the late swing, pace from the wicket, direction and accuracy, were all new experiences. It was plain to Arthur that easy pickings were going to be a rarity when Bedser was in the attack.

These two games were remarkable chiefly for the emphatic return to Test cricket of Don Bradman. In Brisbane he scored 187 after surviving a controversial stroke into the hands of John Ikin in the gully. In short, a bump ball. Ikin and ten other English players were convinced that the ball flew straight from Bradman's bat and was a legitimate catch. Bradman, his partner Hassett and umpire, George Borwick, had another viewpoint. They believed Bradman had chopped the ball into the ground whence it flew straight to gully. Hammond, when passing Don at the end of the over, made some remark the gist of which was that this was not an auspicious start to a Test series. Bradman was 28 at the time and, if given his marching orders, may well have decided to quit the game altogether. In addition, the course of the match may have been radically changed.

At Sydney Barnes and Bradman each scored 234. Barnes was 70 when Don came in at the fall of the fourth wicket at 159. They added 405 before Bradman was out.

I watched the whole of the second Test match from the old Sheridan Stand. Sitting close by me was a typical 'SCG type'—the type usually found on The Hill of joyous memory. When Bradman came out to bat at the fall of the fourth wicket, Sid Barnes, solicitous for his captain's welfare walked half way to the players' gate to meet him. He then apparently briefed Don at some length on the state of play. My friend's dulcet tones had pierced the morning air quite regularly on this sunny day. Watching Barnes expounding matters to Bradman, he called out in a penetrating voice: 'Ah, don't worry about 'im Sid, don't give 'im no drum. 'e knows all about it.' Perhaps only Sid Barnes of those days would have been brash enough to brief Bradman at length on how the situation should be handled. Barnes was a great player—one of the most difficult of his time to dislodge. His occasional antics, considered by some at the time as reprehensible, would scarcely raise an eyebrow today.

In England's second innings Len Hutton set the ground alight with a memorable miniature masterpiece which only yielded 37 runs but lingered long in the memory of those who saw it. Many years later I met, by chance, Colin McCool. Talking of this innings, McCool maintained that Hutton's job was to stay there and forget the fireworks. I remain unconvinced. Not many innings cling to the memory 48 years on—McCabe's 187 n.o., Bradman's hundredth century and Harvey's 92 n.o. in the 1954 Sydney Test are those that come to mind quickly—Hutton's 37 is worthy to be set alongside them, in my view. Australia won these two Tests with ease.

The selectors, adopting the maxim that a batsman of proven class should not be dropped after a couple of failures, stuck to Morris with results that convincingly confirmed both their judgment and Morris's claim to be numbered among the great.

Despite a resounding defeat in the Shield match against Victoria in Melbourne, Morris left his stamp on the match with 83 out of 205 in the first innings, followed by 110 out of 241 in the second. These knocks provided the overture for the third Test match in Melbourne. Bedser claimed him twice, but there was some pain in between successes—21 and 155 earned him general acclaim among the scribes, although Arthur Mailey complained of some slow batting when Bradman joined him in the second innings. O'Reilly, on the other hand, thought Don's 49 his best batting of the series to date. Percy Beames, a Victorian pre-war batsman, excused Morris's slowness by referring to his earlier failures but seemed wide of the mark when he claimed Morris's strokes were fairly limited 'to firm pushes into the covers' or deflections on both sides of the wicket. Most would agree that Arthur was a complete player with drives, cuts, hooks and glances liberally spread throughout his longer stays at the crease. Bedser clean bowled Morris in the second innings and the picture taken at the time suggests Arthur may have left his leg stump exposed, a habit which was to get him into trouble later in his career. O'Reilly already had Arthur in his sights as a future Australian captain and his quiet and calm personality, skill and early assessments of games as they progressed, suggested he would be successful in that role. Cardus was generally approving, commenting that 'Morris is capable of graceful hits to the off and pulls of some splendour, but there is a suspicion of a looseness of technique somewhere'.

By the end of the 1948 tour of England, Neville had revised this observation, which has a somewhat patronising air. His later writings were highly complimentary.

Arthur's Melbourne century was the first by an Australian left-hander in a Melbourne Test since Jack Gregory, batting hatless and gloveless, made 100 in 1921. Arthur had more to show and prove and did what few have done, not even Bradman in a Test match against England, at Adelaide a couple of weeks later, with 122 (c. Evans b. Bedser) and 124 n.o. The 'looseness of technique' suggested by Cardus was less apparent than ever here and one wondered whether Neville had been a little carried away in his earlier pronouncement. While copping some criticism for slow batting in his first innings, his second effort was widely applauded for its splendid strokeplay. Even the acid-ulous Warwick Armstrong could scarce forbear. The match was unusual, not because of any particularly exciting moments, but rather in that Denis Compton joined Morris in making a century in each innings. O'Reilly heaped praise on both, nominating Compton as one of the 'world's greatest modern batsmen' and quoting some English observers who compared Morris with the 'incomparable' Frank Woolley. Bradman had registered a duck in the first innings, and with Australia at 2–18, Morris's circumspection is perhaps understandable. Rightly or wrongly, his position as Australian opener was set in concrete for some years to come. With Sid Barnes, chunky and formidable, they were to be the most effective opening pair Australia had on hand since Woodfull and Ponsford. Unfortunately Barnes's share of the partnership was to be abbreviated somewhat for a variety of reasons and Arthur missed his partner's confidence and determination as time went by. Barnes was always on the look-out for the quick, cheeky single which disconcerted and unsettled opposition bowlers and fieldsmen. Later occupants of the opening position needed a lot of prodding to get them moving which reduced the scoring rate and gave opposing captains fewer wrinkles in the brow area.

Arthur wound up the 1946–47 season with respectable, if not sensational, efforts in the final Test, which was preceded by a Shield match against South Australia and the return match between the MCC and NSW. His season's toil had yielded a rich harvest.

In all first-class games, he totalled 1234 runs at 68.5, and in Test aggregates was second only to Bradman with 503 runs at 71.86. He'd established warm friendships with all his team-mates and enjoyed the company of his opponents. Friendships, especially with Len Hutton, Denis Compton, Bill Edrich and the Bedser twins, were forged which lasted long after cricketing days were done.

Morris's first season in Test cricket compared more than favourably with that of Warren Bardsley, the left-hander with whom he was being compared. Bardsley cut his Test match teeth in England in 1909 when he played in all five matches for an aggregate of 396 at 39.6. Both Morris and Bardsley scored two centuries in a Test match in their first seasons of Test cricket. Bardsley had to contend with a more formidable array of English bowlers than Morris—S F Barnes, Colin Blythe, Wilfred Rhodes and George Hirst would stand up pretty well in any company.

Cricketers were looking forward keenly to the 1947–48 season when a side from India was to visit Australia. This was the first occasion on which a team from the sub-continent had undertaken a Test tour of this country. The visitors expressed pleasure upon learning that Don Bradman was fit and anxious to play in the Tests. In the light of what occurred during the summer, their feelings might have changed slightly by the tour's end. Against an attack which boasted few bowlers of interstate, let alone international, class, the Don had a picnic. After a memorable 172 at Sydney which marked his 100th first-class century, Bradman went on to total 715 at 178.75 in the Tests, with four centuries. In all outings against the visitors, he totalled 1081 runs at 135.12. The Indians certainly had a good look at him and one recalls the complete dominance Bradman displayed after he'd passed his 100th century. The Indians, with seven fieldsmen on the boundary, were completely helpless in stemming the flow of runs. In 28 electric minutes, Bradman added 72 runs, the ball speeding across the turf as if expelled from a gun, leaving fieldsmen pictures of bewildered impotence. Apart from Vinoo Mankad the bowling was mediocre, but Bradman's display was so dazzling that even Bill O'Reilly, never one to lavish unnecessary praise on Bradman, commented that 'there's no answer when Bradman is Bradman'. Mankad, a gifted all-round player, gained some sort of notoriety by running out batsmen who were backing up too far at his end when he was bowling. The couple of such incidents which involved Bill Brown and Rex Rogers were responsible for giving birth to a new cricketing term—'doing a Mankad'. In Lala Amarnath and Vijay Hazare, India had two batsmen of world class. The former was a very useful and accurate bowler despite appearing to bowl off the wrong foot, and he scored heavily on tour in games other than the Tests. Hazare was a magnificent strokeplayer, and scored centuries in each innings of the Adelaide Test. His first-class total of 18 621 runs at 58.19 and 2192 Test runs at 47.65 stamp him as being among the finest players to come out of India.

Morris enjoyed moderate success in the four Tests in which he played against the Indians, although they felt the weight of his bat in the state game against New South Wales. Arthur took the attack apart in making 162 out of his side's 8–561 declared. His Test aggregate of 209 at 52 was modest by comparison with what had preceded it and indeed what was to follow. However, looking at those who played a significant number of innings in the Tests (5), only Bradman and Hassett were ahead of him.

The Australians were far too strong and won four of the five Tests by big margins, averaging 47.74 per wicket against 19.55 by the visitors.

Arthur's form generally was satisfactory with 887 first-class runs at 59.2 with three centuries. He was proving himself a consistent and reliable opener with the redoubtable Barnes. Australian power was approaching the overall strength of Warwick Armstrong's great 1921 side and the 1948 side which Bradman was to lead to England was taking shape. Indeed, of the 18 that played against India, only Bruce Dooland, a class leg-spinner and Len Johnson, medium pace, failed to make the 1948 side.

Bradman's batting skills had faded little. If he was slower to start and some of the more spectacular strokes had been toned down a little, his capacity and appetite for run-making were as great as ever. On some occasions, as in the Sydney match where he notched his 100th first-class century, the brilliance of his stroke play and the uncanny way in which he punctured a runsaving field were scarcely different from his halcyon days.

Only Hassett and Bill Brown, and to a lesser extent Sid Barnes, were on deck from the side Don had led to England in 1938. Stan McCabe had called it a day, O'Reilly had hurled his boots out of the dressing room window at the conclusion of the first-ever Test played by Australia and New Zealand. Ernie McCormick was long past his best, Grimmett scarcely likely to be recalled and Frank Ward, 'Chuck' Fleetwood–Smith, Arthur Chipperfield, Ben Barnett, Merv Waite and Jack Badcock unavailable. Charlie Walker and Ross Gregory had lost their lives in the war. Bradman, it seems, had mellowed and the younger members regarded him with affection as well as awe. Lindsay Hassett had always got on well with him and even if Keith Miller occasionally wanted 'to do his own thing', the post-war sides were without cliques. The war had gone far in eliminating the sectarian bitterness which had been a sad aspect of Australian life in the thirties, spilling over into sport.

Although Arthur appeared certain to be among the early choices for the tour of England during the following northern summer, some supposed weaknesses in his play drew comment from R S Whitington. He observed that Morris, when playing back, did not make full use of the space between the crease and the wicket. This may have been an early symptom of a later malaise, for Morris later in his career was criticised for 'shuffling' across the wicket in back defence rather than moving his left foot across and back—the generally approved method. Some considered that this tendency was leading to his dismissal either by exposure of his leg stump or by his not getting behind deliveries which were moving away off the pitch, leading to slip catches. Whitington's other criticism concerned a perceived failure to get his right foot 'close enough to the ball' when driving through the covers. It should be added that even if valid, this defect did not frequently cause his dismissal.

Morris had shared the New South Wales captaincy duties with Sid Barnes and had carried out the duties in a manner which pleased the critics. Widely admired for his character as well as his cricket, there was speculation that he might be chosen as vice-captain when the 1948 tourists were chosen. It is difficult to see how the selectors could have gone past Hassett for this position. The little man had been a splendid batsman for his state and country. In the pre-war years the effortlessness of his strokemaking suffered little by comparison with Stan McCabe. He had been the only player anywhere to master O'Reilly regularly and the great bowler was prone to display some evidence of frustration when bowling to him. A reporter in the *Sporting Globe* noted that there was 'some opposition on the Board of Control to Hassett holding the position'. If this were so it is difficult to explain on grounds either of ability or character, for Hassett was a widely loved man and his batting ability spoke for itself. Perhaps sectarianism, although dead, was not yet buried.

Morris himself would readily agree that Hassett was the logical choice and so it turned out. Morris was named the third selector for the tour ahead of Bill Brown or Barnes.

This team, rated by many the strongest to leave these shores, was:

BRADMAN D G	SA	(CAPTAIN)
HASSETT A L	VIC	(V-CAPTAIN)
BARNES S G	NSW	
BROWN W A	QLD	
HAMENCE R A	SA	
HARVEY R N	VIC	
JOHNSON I W	VIC	
JOHNSTON W A	VIC	
LINDWALL R R	NSW	

LOXTON S J E	VIC
MCCOOL C L	QLD
MILLER K R	NSW
MORRIS A R	NSW
RING D T	VIC
SAGGERS R A	NSW
TALLON D	QLD
TOSHACK E R H	NSW

There were few surprises. Hamence was a good player at state level with a total output of over 5000 first-class runs at the respectable average of 37.75. His South Australian domicile was probably a key factor in his selection and his chances of gaining a Test match place would be slight except in the event of injury to, or a devastating loss of form by, one of the key players. Bill Johnston's selection surprised some, although he was the fastish left-hand type of bowler who theoretically could be expected to succeed on English wickets. And succeed he did. Moreover he was the ideal tourist and a captain's delight, as he could drop his pace to slow and bowl with equal effect as an orthodox leg spinner. The other marginal choice was Sam Loxton, although he'd scored heavily for Victoria during the season just ended. He proved a great utility man and was an enthusiastic and popular member of the outfit.

Neil Harvey, the infant at 19, owed his selection to a fine century against India which, with his dazzling fielding in any position, persuaded the selectors that he was a good investment for the future. In this they were proved correct and Harvey succeeded so well that he pushed the seasoned and polished Bill Brown out of the Test side before the series ended.

The side's average age was 29 which suggests rightly that for some, the best cricketing years had been swallowed by the war. Keith Johnson was appointed manager.

Len Hutton, shivering in a Yorkshire February, commented: 'It's a very strong side viewed from every angle.' Other English commentators felt England had a reasonable chance of winning the rubber, with Walter Hammond calling for the type of wickets used in the Victory

Tests of 1945. 'Sporting', Hammond called them. In retrospect, one wonders at the mayhem Lindwall, Johnston and Miller may have wrought on 'sporting' wickets.

R S Whitington thought it a strong side, commenting that Miller and Brown were better players in England than Australia. He didn't think that the spin bowlers would trouble England's batsmen. This turned out to be right, but it was because they didn't have to—only Ring played in a Test; the fifth. Whitington thought that Dooland's omission was unfortunate. There appears little doubt that he was the best spinner in Australia and his omission resulted in his loss to our cricket. He took off for England and stayed there.

There was the usual round of farewells. Arthur Morris visited his old school, Canterbury High, and was entertained with Ray Lindwall by the St George Club. After preliminary matches in Tasmania and Western Australia the side was to embark on the 'Strathaird' in Perth on March 19. The first Australian post-war Test tour of England was under way.

Touring

with Bradman

1948

'the greatest Australian side ever?'

THE AUSTRALIANS PLAYED TWO GAMES IN TASMANIA, in the first of which Morris made 33 while Barnes, Harvey and Hassett carved the attack up to the tune of 5 for 538. At Launceston the scoring was not so prolific but Brown and Morris both registered scores in the sixties. Morris's position as opener seemed to be confirmed—in all three games before leaving Australia, he was first in. His partners were Barnes in Hobart and Brown in Launceston and Perth, so that at this stage the second opening spot appeared to be open. Morris's three scores were 33, 61 and 115. Brown made 66 in Launceston and 9 in Perth. Barnes's 111 at Hobart was followed by 11, batting down the list at Launceston. Bradman continued the form he'd shown all summer with 45 and 115. All the bowlers had some success although Miller and Lindwall were obviously being nursed at this stage. McCool took some stick in the West with 2–115 but only one century score was recorded against the visitors in the three games.

The five-week sea trip enabled the players to cement friendships already made or improve some which had been of a casual nature because of differences in domicile. A large contingent of pressmen was on hand, including such notables as Bill O'Reilly and Arthur Mailey. The tourists kept fit with deck sports, running and swimming but, by and large, it was a restful and relaxing time where the main problem was to slacken off the speed with which extra poundage was insidiously creating bulges where no bulge should be.

Bradman, a poor sailor on three previous tours, was not greatly troubled by seasickness but was kept busy putting together the string of speeches he'd be called upon to make in the weeks following his team's arrival in the UK.

In London, the press and public were eagerly awaiting the arrival of the Australians although there was not a great deal of positive thinking as to whether the home side could reverse the beating they'd taken eighteen months before in Australia, and regain the Ashes. The *Daily Mirror* reported that 'luxury suites' had been reserved for Keith Johnson and Bradman at the Piccadilly Hotel while the others 'were quartered two to a room'. Whether or not this was true, at the age of 40 it would be appropriate for the captain to have some privacy, particularly remembering his off field workload of correspondence, speech preparation and so on. As to whether the facility was of a 'luxury' order is another matter and the adjective may have had its birth in the imagination of an enthusiastic reporter.

Landing at Tilbury on April 16, the Australians had almost a fortnight in which to practise before coming to grips with the first tour match against Worcester. This gave them a good period in which to explore the endless places of interest in London—a boon touring teams don't enjoy in these days of air travel. At the Lord's nets the public were admitted at a fairly nominal cost and much interest obviously centred on Bradman. However the players making their first visit came under scrutiny, particularly Arthur Morris, whose deeds had been well reported and who'd taken the bat out on England to some purpose in Australia in 1946. Lindwall and Miller took things fairly quietly and it was evident that Bradman was going to bring his two main strike bowlers along gradually, to peak when the Tests started in early June. There was plenty to see—the two left-handers, Toshack and Johnston, settled into a well defined bowling groove early in the piece and it seemed likely that their workload would be heavy.

Right-arm leg spinners have always been at a premium in England.

One has difficulty in remembering more than three in this century—
'Tich' Freeman, Doug Wright and Eric Hollies spring to mind—after
them, nobody. Consequently McCool and Ring were closely observed,
with the inevitable comparisons being made with Grimmett, Arthur
Mailey and O'Reilly. Neither was as good as any of these three but
they were something of a novelty in a land where finger spin has always
rated higher than the wrist variety. The great Australian leg spinners,
particularly O'Reilly and Grimmett, never relaxed from perfecting their
existing repertoire and adding variations to it. In the home of cricket,
it's been regarded as rather too strenuous when adequate finger spin can
grip on English wickets with less effort and application.

There was a fair amount of campaigning in the English press who
were arguing that Lindwall's 'drag' would be unacceptable to English
umpires. Bradman, when questioned, dealt fairly tersely with this matter,
stating that he didn't expect any trouble and that Lindwall would not
change from his Australian bowling style. The umpires named for the
Australians' game against Leicester were Fred Root and Dai Davies.
Root had been a bowler with Worcester, bowling medium pace leg-
theory to a packed on-side field. Davies was an old Glamorgan cam-
paigner. Bradman chatted briefly to the two before the start of the match
and was apparently satisfied as to their interpretation of the no-ball rule
as it related to 'drag', which was a fault not confined to Ray Lindwall
but was fairly widespread in England at the time.

The Australians had brought with them a large quantity of food
parcels to brighten the lives of English folk who were still severely
rationed nearly three years after the end of the war. Keith Johnson
received many letters from all over the kingdom seeking a cut of the
'goodies'. As these were, of course, limited, Johnson wisely handed them
over to the Ministry of Food for distribution. Johnson's schedule was
hectic and he was frequently busy into the small hours dealing with
correspondence. Social commitments were heavy—dinners, receptions,
cocktail parties, theatre parties and golfing engagements. The Lord
Mayor of London was to entertain them at dinner on the eve of the
Worcester match.

Sid Barnes, ever the non-conformist, had a rubber stamp made of his signature and used this 'signing' autograph books. He enlisted the services of two youngsters to apply the stamp to those books offered for autograph and rewarded them with a steady supply of sweets for their labour. Manager Keith Johnson was not greatly impressed with this entrepreneurial display.

Bradman led a strong side for the first game. Ring, Saggers, Hamence, Loxton and Johnston were omitted and Harvey was 12th man. For Worcester, the old stalwart, R E S Wyatt, was named in the side but took little part in the match.

After bowling the locals out for 233, with McCool and Ian Johnson taking the bowling honours, Morris and Bradman took the Worcester attack apart. Don was content with a modest 107 to set alongside his three double century scores on the previous tours. Morris, who opened with Barnes, was 34 when Bradman came in and beat Don to the century by one run. Bradman's took 145 minutes, Morris's four hours. Arthur earned plaudits from all quarters for his chanceless display which was seen as ideal for an opening batsman. It was certainly a remarkable opening effort under entirely different conditions from those he had previously experienced.

Lindwall and Miller were used sparingly in this match as it was again apparent that Bradman was planning their program with the Tests in view. Englishmen were looking for a bowler of speed with whom to confront the Australians but the search was proving fruitless.

Arthur missed the game against Leicestershire where Keith Miller enjoyed himself to the tune of 202 not out. Doug Ring took five wickets cheaply in one innings and Ian Johnson seven in the other. Maurice Tate was impressed with both but had a pick at Bradman's handling of the bowlers and some of his field placements. Barnes and Bradman had some useful practice against an attack whose main components were two former Sydney players, Vic Jackson and Jack Walsh.

Journeying north to Bradford, where the rain-affected wicket kept scoring to a minimum and brought the greatest batsmen back to the field, Hutton made 5 and 11, Morris 17 and 3 and Miller's 24 in the first innings was the top score for the match. The Australians eventually ran out winners by four wickets, Harvey sealing victory with a six over long-on. Don Bradman, an onlooker, had some anxious moments as his vision of an undefeated tour appeared likely to fade into the Yorkshire murk when Australia had lost 6–47 when chasing 61 in the second innings. Tallon and Harvey proved equal to the challenge.

Against Surrey at the Oval the Australians had a picnic, totalling 632 and bowling the locals out for 141 and 195. Lindwall bowled his first no-ball of the tour in Surrey's first innings, a happening which made headlines in the press. The officiating umpire was Harry Baldwin, a man of some experience in the matter of no-balls—it was he who 'called' Ernie McCormick 35 times in the opening game of the 1938 tour. A sympathetic spectator was consoling McCormick on his misfortune during the lunch break, but McCormick wasn't worried. 'It'll be OK after lunch', he said, 'The umpire's hoarse.' Morris batted soundly for 65 in the Australian innings and, with Barnes, added 136 before Arthur was leg before.

The Cambridge match at lovely Fenners saw another innings win by the Australians. Arthur's contribution was modest but Bill Brown and Lindsay Hassett scored freely. Trevor Bailey, later to be a thorn in the side of Australian teams, was not out 66 in the University's second innings and was described as 'quick footed' and 'brilliant'. These qualities were never especially noticeable in Bailey innings a season or two later. Lindwall had sore legs and was used sparingly, but Colin McCool bowled beautifully to finish with 7–78 in the University's second innings. There can be few more idyllic settings for a cricket match than Fenners, with the University domes and towers close by and the Cam meandering along beside the city. The area is redolent of Rupert Brooke and 'honey for tea', and the wicket has the reputation of being a happy hunting ground for batsmen. Bill Brown certainly found it so on this occasion and proceeded on his stylish unhurried way to a nice round 200. Arthur missed the Essex match which was won by an innings and 451 runs, surely one of the most emphatic wins in cricket history. The total of 721 by the Australians confounded the ancient scoreboard at Southend, there being no provision for number '7' in the hundreds column.

The massacre of counties and universities continued at Oxford where the students went down by an innings and 90 runs. Morris was run out for 64 and Bill Brown was again stating his case for Test selection by the best of all methods—he scored 108. Bill O'Reilly was critical of Toshack who was concentrating his attack well wide of the leg stump—many of these deliveries would be ignored by experienced players. However, Toshack captured the expatriate Australian, B H (Jika) Travers, cheaply in both innings.

MCC picked a strong side to meet the Australians at Lord's with Hutton, Edrich and Compton supported by a New Zealander, Martin Donnelly, and some prospective Test match bowlers in Jim Laker, Jack Young and Ken Cranston. It was of little avail. Significantly, Bradman chose Barnes to open with Morris, dropping Bill Brown to No 6 where he was barracked for slow play.

Arthur made only 5 before being lbw to part-time 'fast' bowler, Bill Edrich. Bradman's dismissal at 98 caused much comment and the scribes were busily looking for the last occasion when Don had been sent marching when so close to his century. It was a dazzling 98, however, and the 33 000 fans were well pleased. Don Bradman was as much appreciated in England as he was at home in Australia. English cricket lovers like to get value for money and Bradman was consistently able to provide it. As a Test trial, the match could not have solved many problems for the English selectors, but the probable Australian side was taking shape.

Arthur Morris was having a lean trot hereabouts and his luck didn't change at Old Trafford against Lancashire, where Dick Pollard had him twice for 22 and 5. A 19-year-old, left-hand slow spinner, Malcolm Hilton, caused some surprise and wrote himself into the county's list of immortals by capturing Bradman twice for 43 and 11. One wondered what the youngster's fate might be should he encounter Don again on tour. The game was drawn. Lindwall was now nearing his peak and getting through his fair share of overs. Bill Johnston was proving the success of the tour. He captured wickets regularly and presented a variety of problems to batsmen.

Lindwall finally hit his straps, the occasion, fittingly, being the match against Notts at Trent Bridge. The Trent Bridge turf had thundered to the boots of Larwood and Voce in the not-so-distant past and

Lindwall, so similar in run-up and action to Larwood, left his mark with 6 for 14 from 15 overs. Probably Lindwall was marginally less fast than Larwood, but at around 150 kmh the difference is not terribly significant. Lindwall's arm was a little lower than Larwood's at delivery but apart from that, film of the two shown one beneath the other reveals a startling similarity. In this Trent Bridge match, the home players adhered strictly to the forward prod, with disastrous results. Reg Simpson, a stylish player, made a good 74 and with 'young Joe' Hardstaff added 98 runs for the third wicket, but other than that, the score sheet made dismal reading. Simpson and Hardstaff were similar in style, both being wristy players with high grips on the bat.

Arthur was still in the batting doldrums and was leg before to Jepson for 16. But his time was drawing closer.

At Hove, happy hunting ground of Maurice Tate and Arthur Gilligan, Lindwall was again in devastating form, taking 6–34 and 5–25. The county players had no answer to the speed and fire of the great bowler. After Bill Brown was out for 44, Morris and Bradman added 189 for the second wicket and, after Harvey notched up an even 100, Bradman closed the innings at 5–549. Of the opening partnership between Brown and Morris, Bill Brown scored 44 of the 153 recorded. This gives some idea of the brilliance of the left-hander's innings of 184.

The Australians returned to Nottingham for the first Test match. The side virtually picked itself, the only queries being whether Barnes or Brown would open with Morris?—and if Barnes, could Brown hold his place ahead of Harvey or Loxton? In the event, Harvey was omitted and Brown included and dropped to No 6 in the batting order—an indication of the strength of this side. At the end of the war, Bill Brown would have been widely regarded as the best batsman in Australia with the inevitable exception of D G Bradman. He led the Australians on the short tour of New Zealand at the end of 1945–46 home season, and had Bradman elected not to play in 1946–47, would almost certainly have been chosen, subject to fitness, to lead his country against Hammond's Englishmen. As it happened, he missed all the 1946–47 Tests due to illness but was an automatic choice against the Indians and would have been one of the first picked of the present touring party.

The match was one-sided. The Englishmen batted badly in the first innings. Morris was bowled off his pads by Laker, and Bradman and Hassett scored undistinguished centuries. Compton played magnificently for 184 in the second innings before falling on his wicket when trying to avoid a bumper from Miller. With a new ball available after 55 overs, the Australians were on velvet and their three fast bowlers made the most of this very bad aberration in the rules. Miller was hooted roundly for what was seen as an excess of bumpers and one wondered what would have happened had England been equipped with similar fire power. Australia won by 8 wickets after Morris was clean bowled by Bedser for 9 and Bradman turned the same bowler into Hutton's hands at leg gully for zero. Bedser had profited from some gratuitous advice from Bill O'Reilly on his field settings and must have been well pleased with the first dividends.

The comprehensive defeat caused consternation in the corridors of the MCC, to say nothing of the press and public. But there were redeeming features. The two giants of English cricket, Compton and Hutton, had withstood all that could be thrown at them in the second innings of 441, and Alec Bedser had bowled with great heart and skill. It had taken 216 long overs for the Australians to reach their total of 509, the only bowler who yielded easier runs being part-time operator Bill Edrich. On the other hand, it was plain that the Englishmen were opposed to a side which batted down to no 9—the occupant of this batting position being R R Lindwall, a Test century maker in Australia in 1946–47. The Australian bowling had more variety and penetration, with two of the greatest fast bowlers of any time, supported by a left-hander who gave nothing away whether bowling fast or slow, and orthodox left-hand and right-hand spinners who were difficult to subdue. At wicket-keeping parity was reached—it would be hard to separate Tallon and Godfrey Evans.

Arthur played in the match against Northampton and made 60. He missed the Yorkshire match at Bramall Lane, Sheffield, where Bradman again was trapped by Hutton at leg gully, this time off the bowling of Aspinall, for a second innings 86. Barnes failed twice but Bill Brown notched another century in the second innings. He certainly was demonstrating again his capacity and appetite for runs on English wickets. This match, which preceded the Lord's Test, was drawn.

The Lord's Test, high point of the English cricketing summer, was of special significance in that it was to be Don Bradman's final Test appearance at the famous ground. Morris made a splendid first innings 105 after Barnes' early exit and watched while his captain weathered some very good bowling by Laker and Bedser. The latter had him again at leg gully—for 38—Hutton and 30 000 others could scarcely believe what their eyes saw.

Jack Fingleton had expressed some concern at a recent tendency by Arthur Morris to shuffle across the crease rather than utilise the space between crease and stumps when playing back. In this innings Arthur corrected this fault, at least temporarily, and delighted the crowd with a classical display of strokes to all points, including a six off Jim Laker. Arthur's century was his fourth against England in only seven Tests and he found himself in illustrious company—Warwick Armstrong, Sid Gregory, Clem Hill and Stan McCabe. All these had taken many more Tests to register the number—Armstrong 42 matches, Gregory 52, Hill 41, McCabe 24. But surely these statistics can be misleading—it would be fallacious to claim that Morris was so much a greater player than Hill or McCabe. Barnes scored the Lord's century he'd promised himself on the way over and Len Hutton had a bad match. He was peppered with a spate of bumpers in poor light in the second innings and was plainly uncomfortable against the lifting ball. Morris's second innings 62 was in similar vein to his first innings and was ended by a short ball from Doug Wright which he missed when attempting to swing it to leg. Bradman made a sound 89 in the second innings and seemed to be pursuing his calm inevitable way to a final Lord's century when he fell again at the hands of Bedser, but this time to a brilliant diving slip catch by Edrich. In the end the Australians ran out easy winners by the substantial margin of 409 runs. There was alarm and despondency among Englishmen and the press did not spare individuals. Yardley came in for criticism and the home side's batting was rightly described as fairly purposeless. Drastic remedies were called for and were heeded, not altogether wisely, as we shall see.

Morris missed the return match against Surrey but at Bristol against Gloucestershire, in a batting avalanche, he tore the unfortunate county bowlers, including the widely esteemed off spinner Tom Goddard, to tatters. In a Bradmanesque performance, he scored centuries in each of the first two sessions of play, and the entire innings of 290 occupied only five hours and included 40 fours and one six.

After scoring a century in his first Test match appearance at Lord's, cricket's Mecca, Arthur was 'on top of the world' when he went east to Bristol and encountered the unfortunate Tom Goddard. He'd observed that Jim Laker was getting a bit of stick, both from the Australian batsmen and the English press, some of whose scribes were advocating Laker's replacement by Tom Goddard for the Manchester Test. Arthur recalls, 'After we got through the new ball on came Tom. And I went after him. When he bowled to an offside field, I hit him to the on side. When he bowled to a leg field, I hit him through the off field or lofted him. I was on a high and really did have the bowling by the scruff of the neck. On reaching 290, I thought "wouldn't it be nice to get 300" and then promptly hit a full toss back to the bowler. I just lost concentration. Neil Harvey and Sam Loxton further ripped Goddard apart and that was the last we read of his taking over from Jim'.

Ian Johnson had a picnic with the ball taking 11 wickets in the match. Charlie Barnett, who'd played in the Trent Bridge Test, failed twice but Jack Crapp scored an unbeaten century in the first innings which was to earn him a Test spot at Old Trafford.

The Old Trafford Test was notable (or infamous) for one of the monumental selection errors of Test history. In a move which caused anger and dismay all over the Kingdom, but particularly in his home county of Yorkshire, the moguls of the MCC dropped Hutton. He had batted poorly at Lord's, particularly in the second innings in murky light with Lindwall bouncing two or three deliveries at his head in each over. But as Jack Fingleton noted, Hutton in his past seven Test innings against Australia had totalled 402 runs at 67, including a classic 122 at Sydney in 1947 when he was forced to retire ill. The Australians, who regarded Hutton as the best player in England—the one whose wicket they valued more than any other—were staggered.

The match was drawn. Compton played another splendid innings and, with Alec Bedser, added 121 runs for the eighth wicket. England performed much more creditably in the match and may well have won had not Manchester weather intervened. Morris made 51 in the first innings and was 54 not out when the match petered out.

The Old Trafford Test had been England's best performance in the series so far despite the absence of Hutton. They had actually led Australia on the first innings and, but for rain, might have run out winners, although Bradman and Morris were looking menacing in the second innings.

Morris was in the runs against Middlesex where his century put him within range of Bradman's tour aggregate of 1444. Morris had 1316 runs at 69.26, Bradman 1444 at 80.22. Australia ran out winners by 10 wickets. A lively century by Sam Loxton assured him of a place in the Leeds Test.

The Headingley ground at Leeds had been an unfortunate one for England—of the eight Tests played there, Australia had won three and five had been drawn. It was the ground that Bradman had virtually made his own with two triple centuries and a modest single century in 1938. He was destined yet again to play a significant matchwinning part in the contest now about to begin.

The England selectors recalled Hutton and brought in Cranston for Dollery. The absence of a left-arm spinner was to prove vital in the end when, with the wicket crumbling and Laker collared, Yardley was reduced to part-timers Compton and Hutton to provide some spin backup. Both were punished heavily. England scored well in both innings, Hutton delighting his home crowd with runs in both innings. In the final innings Australia were set 404 runs to win in 345 minutes. After losing Hassett early, the task appeared impossible but Morris and Bradman set about an inadequate England attack and achieved a memorable victory by 7 wickets. Bradman was 173 not out at the end, Morris falling just before the finish for 182. O'Reilly wrote that Morris was 'one of the greatest left-hand batsmen of all time'. Few in England or Australia would have quibbled at this. Bradman's 173 not out lifted his total Leeds' Test runs to 963. Morris's innings was 'enchanting' according to Jack Fingleton and the winning of a game in the conditions existing was a remarkable achievement. One wonders what would have been the result if England had had a bowler like Hedley Verity, Wright or Hollies to support Laker on a pitch which should have suited spin bowlers admirably. Laker failed to take a wicket and had 93 runs taken from his 32 overs. Adequate spin support at the other end may well have seen a different result. Those who saw Laker bowl later in his career, notably in 1956 in England when he wrought havoc among Ian Johnson's side and later in Australia in 1958 when he bowled quite beautifully, would find it hard to relate the latter-day Laker to the 1948 edition. Then he appeared to present an ideal target for hits for six out of the small English grounds.

In a later interview, Morris added a bit of background to the newspaper accounts of this innings at Headingley. He said that the English papers' assumption that a home victory was a virtual certainty, and that the game would be finished shortly after lunch at the latest, put his back up and persuaded him to prove them wrong. He knew that the England captain had to go for a win following the losses at Trent Bridge and Lord's. Morris knew also that the spin component at Yardley's disposal was limited—a bowler like Doug Wright to support Laker would have put an entirely different complexion on the struggle; but unfortunately, Doug Wright whom the Australians considered to be, apart from Bedser, the best bowler in England, was busy in a match with his Kent County team. Bradman also was not without hope of a win. Arthur took risks to knock Compton out of the attack and Laker had some distance to go before he reached his best form some seasons later. The dusty wicket did not suit the quicker bowlers and the introduction of Hutton into the attack was a desperate and costly measure. Arthur said that Bradman was, as ever, quick and decisive between the wickets and took a heavy toll of the attack after Compton had been dealt with. It was indeed a famous victory.

Arthur Morris had a quieter period following the Leeds Test but the side continued on its winning way. Bradman took another century against Lancashire, his eighth of the tour.

Although the rubber had been decided and the Ashes were to

remain in Australia's keeping, there was a lot of interest in the final Test to be played at the Oval in London. England's batting had improved match by match and loyal Englishmen were hoping that they might take the final game. This was a forlorn hope. On a damp wicket, a dismal 52 was all their heroes could put together. Hutton was last man out for 30 in this debacle. Lindwall had his best ever Test figures of 6–20 from 16 overs and the whole sorry procession lasted only about two hours. Morris and Barnes gave the Australians a sound start but after Barnes left, Morris held the side together only to be run out when 196. Maurice Tate described his innings as 'magnificent' with strokes to all parts of the field.

Neville Cardus, who judged left-handers by the yardstick of the incomparable Frank Woolley, was sufficiently moved to congratulate Morris in prose worthy of his appreciation of Stan McCabe a decade earlier:

'Morris once more was beyond praise—masterful, stylish, imperturbable, sure in defence, quick and handsome in stroke play. His batting is true to himself, charming and good mannered but reliant and thoughtful.

'Seldom does he spare a ball of suspicious character, yet he is never palpably acquisitive, never brutal. He plunders bowlers tastefully and changes rubbish to cultured art.

'I never tire of watching him.'

The Oval innings gave him 696 runs in the Tests at 87, which put him just ahead of Barnes, 329 at 82 and Bradman 508 at 72.57.

Eric Hollies had left an indelible mark on the record books with his second-ball dismissal of Bradman and finished with the excellent figures of 5–131 off 56 overs. Australia won by an innings and 149 runs to take the rubber 4–0. The 1938 Oval massacre had been well and truly avenged.

With the Tests over the tour was winding down, the main consideration being to ensure that Bradman's last tour of England should not be marred by a defeat at the eleventh hour. The Australians went down to the lovely Canterbury ground, so long graced by the matchless Frank Woolley. His successors did little to honour his past deeds and could muster only 51 and 124 in reply to the Australians' 361. Godfrey Evans caught Arthur after a bright 43 and Bill Brown registered another century in his own classical and unhurried style.

Arthur Mailey, in a despatch from London, drew comparisons between Armstrong's 1921 side and the present combination. 'Out of the melting pot', his combined side was: Bradman (Captain), Morris, Barnes, Bardsley, C G Macartney, Miller, Jack Gregory, Lindwall, Armstrong, Oldfield, Mailey, Harvey (12th). This side had only one tailender (Mailey), and would have scored thousands. It would be rich in genuine all-rounders—Miller, Gregory, Armstrong and Macartney. Speed and spin would be well served and the batsmen would have style, solidity and aggression in equal proportions.

Returning to Lord's, Arthur had a rest while his colleagues gave the 'Gentlemen' a most ungentlemanly leather hunt. Brown scored his eighth tour century at the respectable rate of 47 per hour, and both Bradman and Hassett flayed a fairly ordinary attack.

Arthur was still resting for the Somerset game at Taunton and the match against South of England at Hastings. Runs were easily come by in both places. The first-class fixtures were to be completed in the game against Leveson–Gower's eleven at Scarborough. Although the home side included players like Hutton, Edrich, Martin Donnelly, Bedser and Laker, they were mauled by Bradman's men, the Don delighting the crowd with his eleventh century of the tour to finish top of the aggregate and average against all comers. Arthur scored 62, falling 78 runs short of 2000 for the tour. Had he achieved this goal he would have joined Bradman in being the only players to do so on their first visit to England.

There can be some argument that this side was the best to tour England from Australia. The only other candidate is Armstrong's 1921 side. Both combinations took England on shortly after devastating wars from which British people were still only slowly recovering. Having said that, Bradman's was an exceptionally well balanced team which was assisted by the new rule which allowed a new ball after 55 overs. This suited Lindwall and his bowling partners and Bradman correctly made full use of the law. Sadly, it marked the beginning of the end for spin bowlers. In 1991—43 years later—we found the Australian captain and selectors begging a fairly run-of-the-mill leg spinner, Trevor Hohns, to come out of retirement to bolster the spinning department. McCool, Ring and Johnson in Bradman's side took their sidelining in good part for the greater good of the cause but, with hindsight, the victories of 1948 reveal rather more sombre implications for the game. Recently a new star has appeared in the person of Shane Warne.

Arthur Morris, with 696 runs at 87, headed the Test aggregate and average. These figures are remarkable for a man on his first tour of England. In 1989 another left-hander from New South Wales came close to equalling them. Mark Taylor scored 839 in six Tests at the average of 83.9. The comparison is worth recording:

	M	I	NO	Runs	H/S	50	100	Avge
Morris	5	9	1	696	196	3	3	87
Taylor	6	11	1	839	219	5	2	83.90

The two series in which the men played were characterised by heavy defeats of England by the Australians. The parlous state of England's cricket in 1989 (painfully confirmed in Australia in 1991, but in 1994 showing signs of rebirth) is high-lighted by the fact that no fewer than 19 bowlers were used. The most successful was Neil Foster with 12 wickets at 35.08. In 1948 England called on 14 bowlers, the best of whom was Alec Bedser with 18 wickets at 38.22. In 1989, six Australians had batting averages above 50, in 1948 only four. The differences in quality between bowlers encountered would be fairly small, but one tends to think Taylor may have had some slight advantage.

There were a couple of lighthearted games against Scotland at Edinburgh and Aberdeen. With Scotland 3–40 in the Edinburgh game, Bradman threw the ball to Morris who completely bamboozled the Caledonians with his left-hand off spinners, a phenomenon as yet unknown in these latitudes. In five overs he took 5–10. At one stage he had 5–2, but his analysis was spoilt by two lusty boundaries from the bat of a spare, lanky Scot when Morris sent down two orthodox deliveries for variety. And that was it. Thoughts of home were now uppermost and after a visit to Balmoral as guests of King George VI and Queen Elizabeth, the 1948 Australians headed south.

Prelude to
South Africa
AT HOME
1948–49

a season to 'tune-up'

BRADMAN'S 1948 TOURISTS RETURNED HOME to a domestic season uninterrupted by any visit from overseas cricketers. It was to be a special season if only because it would see the final exit of Don Bradman from the game he'd adorned for more than 20 years. He had not intended to play again even for his club but was persuaded to turn out for three testimonial matches—one for himself in Melbourne, one in Sydney for Alan Kippax and Bert Oldfield and a Sheffield Shield match which was held as a testimonial for Arthur Richardson in Adelaide.

There was some early speculation that Morris might be in line for the Australian captaincy. It was difficult though, to see how, in justice, the selectors could go past Lindsay Hassett both on personal and cricketing grounds.

Arthur was appointed captain of New South Wales and started the season in fine style against Queensland in Brisbane with 120 made in 210 minutes. He and Miller flayed the Queensland attack, Miller's 109 occupying only 137 minutes with three sixes and ten fours. There was some criticism of the New South Wales team when the game petered out tamely on the final day after the visitors had obtained first innings points. Statistics of the match suggest that the home team was primarily responsible due to the slow run rate in their second innings. After New South Wales finished on 499 in even time, the Queenslanders occupied the crease for nearly two full days in totalling 384. This did not offer the visitors much incentive to make a game of it, although the incidence of 'blistered feet' in four New South Wales players makes one wonder if there were some collusion as well as resentment at the Queenslanders' dilatoriness which kept their guests for 12 hours in the field under the northern sun.

In his own testimonial match Bradman scored his almost inevitable century in the first innings but fell for 10 to a catch at the wicket from Bill Johnston's bowling in the second innings. Arthur was in his best form with 108 in the second innings in 135 minutes. Watching him bat at this time one was struck by the ease and variety of his strokeplay and the deceptive power with which he dealt with bowlers of all types. Charts of his bigger innings show the all-round versatility of his play. Driving, cutting or hooking, he was a delight to the eye. For an opener he rarely knuckled under to allow bowlers to call the tune and when facing slow bowlers would dance down the wicket to hit high and hard down the ground. His placing was first class and, if he possessed the traditional strength on the leg side which has usually characterised left-handers, these strokes did not dominate his play to the exclusion of classical drives and cuts. Watching Mark Taylor at his best one thinks of Arthur Morris—he has most of Arthur's off side strokes but seemed for a time to have disowned the hook and pull which he used so well in England in 1989. With fast bowlers spearing the ball consistently in towards his body, he has now resurrected these strokes, the hook particularly. Morris said recently that he can't recall ever being out to a fast bowler coming around the wicket. Quick footed, he could get inside the line and help the ball on its way. Lately Taylor seems at times to forsake his successful backfoot play for the forward prod. The uncharitable may see the influence of Australian Test coach Bob Simpson at work again here. Speaking of Simpson, Arthur considers Mark Taylor the finest slip fieldsman since the Australian coach was pocketing them nonchalantly a few years ago.

In Perth, after being dropped first ball, Arthur went on to score

163 in a knock described, by that hackneyed word, as 'brilliant'. New South Wales won outright easily. He was cut back to size a little in Adelaide with 12 and 61, falling twice to Geoff Noblet. Noblet was a splendid fast-medium bowler, denied a regular Test spot by Lindwall, Miller and Johnston.

In Melbourne, on a lively wicket suitable to Bill Johnston's fastish left-hand deliveries, Arthur gave the locals another virtuoso display with 177, more than half the New South Wales side's first innings total of 334. By the time the New South Wales team returned to Sydney, Morris, Lindwall, Saggers and Miller had travelled 6200 miles by air since the Bradman testimonial match in Melbourne five weeks previously. In today's terms, this does not seem exceptional but in 1949 it was viewed with amazement.

Back at the Sydney Cricket Ground for the New Year match against Queensland, rain reduced playing time but not sufficiently to prevent another Morris century—108 not out before lunch in the second innings, completed in 82 minutes. His partner, Jim Burke, made 29 in the session. Morris considers that, in matches other than Tests, this innings was the best he played. Pulls, hooks and drives all featured in the innings which Bill Brown, the Queensland skipper, described as one of the finest he'd seen on the Sydney Cricket Ground. Bill added that Morris's hooking was the best he'd seen since Stan McCabe. Morris recalls that Len Johnson, a medium-pace Queensland bowler, obliged by bowling bouncers to him which, coming nicely off a still grassy wicket, simply asked to be hooked. Brown considered Arthur superior as an opener to Len Hutton because of his devastating hooking ability. Keith Miller bracketed him with Denis Compton 'as the best two batsmen in the world'.

Bill Brown had first encountered Morris in a friendly game against St Joseph's College in Sydney before the war. Stan McCabe took the side out to his old school and sent Morris in to open the innings with Brown. In a letter, Bill Brown wrote: 'It wasn't long before he began to cart the bowlers in all directions with some of the most beautifully timed shots I had ever seen'. Bill, a graceful and prolific player himself, remembers thinking that the best thing he could do was to get out as soon as possible to terminate invidious comparisons between himself, an international cricketer, and an unknown stripling freshly out of school.

Arthur's good run came to a temporary halt in the return game against Victoria in Sydney. He fell twice to the left-arm all-rounder, Harry Lambert for 1 and 2. Lambert's Sheffield Shield career was brief and he soon found his way to the Lancashire League. Bowling in tandem with another fastish left-hander, Bill Johnston, they would have been a formidable pair.

Johnston was an earlier edition of today's Bruce Reid. Both were tall men—Johnston perhaps three or four inches shorter than Reid. Both bowled a lively fast–medium. Johnston tended to swing into the right-handed batsmen, keeping his away-swinger as a shock delivery. He bowled it beautifully. Reid, on the other hand, concentrated, at least in the summer of 1990–91, on slanting five out of six deliveries across the batsman towards slips against England. His success with these tactics bordered on the sensational, although most of his victims connived at their own ruin by hitting across the line when playing forward. They never seemed to learn from earlier mistakes and kept on with the same tactics until it seemed almost ritualistic self-immolation. Bill Johnston was a captain's delight for he could, when called upon, drop his pace and bowl orthodox left-hand spin. In both capacities he was successful. In 40 Tests he took 160 wickets at 23.91. As batsmen, both Reid and Johnston slotted comfortably into the No 11 position, Bill perhaps being a superior performer by a hair's breadth. In England in 1953, all the Australians took part in Lindsay Hassett's scheme to see Bill top of the tour averages. Batting last throughout, Johnston's final figures were: 16 M, 17 I, 16 n.o. 102 runs—average 102.

Morris's setback was temporary and he was back in the runs with another century against South Australia and 66 in the Kippax–Oldfield testimonial in Sydney. The two beneficiaries of this game were among the elite of New South Wales and Australian cricket. Kippax had been a player of supreme elegance, a prolific rungetter in State cricket and a much loved and respected man. In one of the selectors' occasional super-blunders, he'd been left out of the Australian touring team of 1926—a year when Kippax was at the peak of his considerable powers. Bertie

Oldfield was the wicket-keeper par excellence. Cardus called him the 'Claude Duval of wicket-keepers', so unobtrusive, polite and almost apologetic was he as he stumped or caught his victims. He was equally at home taking Jack Gregory and Ted McDonald or Grimmett and O'Reilly. Immaculate and precise, his walk between wickets at the end of each over had a character of its own as he pushed and padded his gloved fingers to ensure that the tips were firmly lodged in the right place. He rarely appealed, and when he did the batsman usually departed without glancing at the umpire for Bertie was punctilious in observing what he saw as the ethics of a great game. This attitude is not especially noticeable today.

Bill O'Reilly tells a story of his own trust in Bertie's infallibility when the 1935–36 Australians returned from South Africa. A match was arranged between the touring side and the Rest of Australia at Sydney as a testimonial for Warren Bardsley and Jack Gregory. The tourists, skippered by Victor Richardson 'lent' Leo O'Brien to Bradman's side. Affairs were so arranged that Bradman would bat on the Saturday afternoon, ensuring a good crowd and a considerably better 'gate'. O'Reilly, in devastating form, dismissed the first three of Bradman's side in no time at all. The organisers had held the Don back rather than expose him to a rampaging 'Tiger', but finally had to send him in when the fourth wicket fell shortly before lunch. Vic Richardson, reluctantly but in the interests of the two beneficiaries, had to take O'Reilly off. Bradman went on to get 212, giving all bowlers a hiding, including O'Reilly. When Bradman was about 90 and apparently holding a 99-year lease of the crease, O'Reilly came back into the attack. He thought he detected a faint snick down the leg side early in this spell, the ball being taken with his usual neatness by Bertie standing up at the stumps. Bertie did not appeal and, working on the established infallibility of Oldfield in these matters, Bill O'Reilly choked off the tentative enquiry he was about to make. At the tea adjournment 'Mo' O'Brien, who was batting with Bradman, said to Bill: 'Didn't you want to get the little bloke out?' O'Reilly, nonplussed, replied: 'What do you mean?' O'Brien replied that, in his opinion, Don had certainly nicked the delivery in question and would probably have been given the push if anyone had appealed. This appalling lapse haunted Bill to his dying day.

Arthur Morris, in the Australian summer of 1948–49 in nine first-class games, scored 1069 runs at 66.81 with six centuries and two fifties. In sixteen completed innings he passed 50 on eight occasions, a performance of almost Bradmanesque proportions.

The 1948 tour of England and the following Australian summer probably marked the zenith of Arthur Morris's batting. Although he was destined to play many further innings of top quality and value, these early seasons after the long frustrating lay-off of the war years found him playing cricket worthy of the select top half dozen all-time Australian greats. Hill, Macartney, McCabe and Trumper would contentedly allow him a place beside them. He was the complete opening batsman—aggressive when aggression was appropriate, solid when the situation called for care. Batting with Bradman, he suffered little by comparison.

Ian Johnson has stated that he shares top billing with Gary Sobers as the finest left-handers Johnson saw. Ian says: 'He always had so much time to play his shots. He watched the ball more closely than most and invariably played late [ie off the back foot]. Like McCabe, he caressed the ball rather than hit it, yet it sped on its way with incredible speed, so correct was his timing.'

Arthur was not only a dry wicket exponent. Ian Johnson recalls opening the second innings with Morris in the 1948 Manchester Test after Sid Barnes had been laid low in the field by a violent pull shot from the bat of Dick Pollard. 'There had been a little rain and the pitch was just a bit responsive. Arthur took strike to Alec Bedser who moved the ball both ways in the air and off the pitch. He hit every ball of that first over in the middle. At the end of the over he came down the pitch and said: "It's doing a bit. We'd better stick around or Alec will run through us." ' Johnson was more than happy to agree with Arthur's suggestion that he (Morris) face Bedser, as Johnson felt that he'd have 'no hope' against him in his present spell.

Morris and he hung on for about an hour during which time the wicket improved slightly, but, more significantly, Johnson did not face one ball from Bedser. 'It was fantastic,' says Johnson, 'to watch the way Morris handled everything Alec Bedser could hurl at him from an extensive repertoire.' Ian Johnson adds that Morris frequently shielded his partners but did it in a 'most unobtrusive way'.

The Australian season of 1948–49 was rather special because players' performances were likely to be closely scrutinised with a view to assessing prospects for the tour of South Africa which was scheduled for the following season (1949–50). In 'The Union' as it was then known, speculation was rife regarding the composition of the touring side. The question of bumpers was given a good airing, with the inclusion of three fast bowlers considered likely. The Springboks had their own far from indifferent fast bowler in Cuan McCarthy who'd not spared the Englishmen in the previous African season. The Australian Cricket Board announced that the tourists would be paid an 'allowance' of £450 for 'out of pocket expenses'. The fact that those chosen would be absent from their usual work for at least four months carried little weight with our administrators. Nobody quibbled at a sum which would now provoke a large guffaw if offered to our present heroes. Those honoured by selection to represent their country had to make the best arrangements they could with employers or relatives to support them and, in some cases, wives and families during their absence.

Before the touring party was announced, Arthur was embarrassed by rumours that he might be in contention for the captaincy. To him it was unthinkable that Hassett could be bypassed for the position. Hassett was extremely popular among all the cricketing fraternity, had served as vice-captain under Bradman with distinction, and had provided a link between captain and 'crew'. It appears that Hassett only secured the job by the odd vote in 13 Board members. Perhaps the legacy of sectarianism, so prevalent in Australian society before World War II, was still alive, even if in its death throes. Arthur was relieved when Hassett was finally appointed and he, a Protestant, was happy to serve under the captain and manager who were both Catholics.

The fourteen players chosen were fairly predictable but, when the side was announced, there was surprise and indignation at the omission of Keith Miller, widely regarded as the finest all-round cricketer in the world. Miller had had a fairly indifferent domestic season and appeared a little tired after the England tour. The player who replaced him, Sam Loxton, had plundered runs all around the land, had picked up a few wickets with his fast-medium tearaway bowling and was a fine fieldsman. He proved an admirable replacement and an excellent tourist.

Those chosen were:

HASSETT A L	VIC	(CAPTAIN)
MORRIS A R	NSW	(V-CAPTAIN)
ARCHER K A	QLD	
HARVEY R N	VIC	
JOHNSON I W	VIC	
JOHNSTON W A	VIC	
LANGLEY G R A	SA	
LINDWALL R R	NSW	
LOXTON S J E	VIC	
McCOOL C L	QLD	
MORONEY J A R	NSW	
NOBLET G J	SA	
SAGGERS R A	NSW	
WALKER A K	NSW	

Moroney was the replacement for Sid Barnes who had called it a day after a couple of disagreements with officialdom which, by today's standards, would scarcely rate a mention in the press. Moroney was a prolific scorer in State matches but few people would put him in the same class as Barnes. The pace bowling would be shared between Lindwall, Noblet and the two left-handers, Walker and Johnston. Alan Walker, a dual international in rugby and cricket, was very fast indeed but was kept out of Test sides by Lindwall and Miller. Tallon and Saggers were beyond criticism as the two leading Australian wicket-keepers, while the spinning was left to McCool (leg break) and Ian Johnson (off break). Tallon, unfortunately, had to withdraw and was replaced by South Australian Gil Langley. Sam Loxton came in for Miller and Ken Archer was the third opener. The side was well enough balanced with five specialist batsmen, four specialist bowlers, two genuine all-rounders in Loxton and McCool, and two who might easily qualify as capable all-rounders in Lindwall and Ian Johnson.

The omission of Miller prompted Alan Kippax and Stan McCabe to remark that 'any side that can afford to drop Miller at the present time must, of necessity, be tremendously strong'. Ironically, the Board had to send Miller over later, following an injury to Bill Johnston. The other contentious matter in the selection was that the selectors considered fourteen players an adequate number to tour. This was the same number as had toured with Victor Richardson in 1935–36.

E A (Chappie) Dwyer was appointed Manager. Dwyer was a figure of some stature and experience and was a popular choice. With Lindsay Hassett as captain, the omens were favourable for a happy tour.

Happy Days
'On the Veldt'
SOUTH AFRICA
1949–50

the 'Post Bradman Era' begins

THE AUSTRALIANS LEFT THESE SHORES on September 17, 1949, aboard the SS *Nestor*, the proposed tour having been extended to 25 matches between late October 1949 and mid-March 1950. Bill O'Reilly, writing in the *Sydney Morning Herald*, gave South Africa an accolade for their contribution to spin bowling, around the turn of the century, in the person of Ernie Vogler whom Bill numbered among the greatest leg spinners of all time. Predictably, Bill went on to lament the fact that this Australian side boasted only one leg spinner—Colin McCool.

South African dailies allotted miles of column inches to the impending tour. Veteran Bruce Mitchell, now aged 40, had come in for some vigorous criticism following his slow batting against the touring Englishmen the year before. Calls for younger players abounded, but the hard facts were that four 'veterans' had headed the batting averages against England—Dudley Nourse 536 runs at 76, Eric Rowan 319 at 53, Mitchell 475 at 52, W W Wade 407 at 50. The Australians would have been more than happy to see any one of that quartet omitted from the South African Test side. The Johannesburg *Sunday Times* pointed out that J B Hobbs ended his Test career at age 48, Sutcliffe 41 and Hammond 43, and that selections should be based on form rather than age.

Arriving in Durban on 7 October, Chappie Dwyer and Lindsay Hassett at once set the tone for an harmonious visit by their willingness to talk to pressmen and the public. Hassett had, just before the team left, been presented with his second child, another girl. The little man was clearly delighted and his good humour had spread to all members of the party. Hassett was not overwhelmed by the fact that this was, from an Australian point of view, a new era in our cricket—the 'post-Bradman era'. Bradman had dominated the scene for 20 years and a lesser man than Hassett might have been a little subdued by this fact.

Dudley Nourse was among those who greeted the Australians, and pictures taken on the occasion reflect the goodwill which was to be the hallmark of this tour. Hassett replied to Nourse's greeting by saying: 'How are you Dudley? I hope you are not feeling too well.' Hassett and Morris had shared a cabin on the trip over and had established an easy relationship—not difficult with people of this calibre.

Bad weather delayed net practice for the Australians, but at early functions the captain and manager made excellent impressions and the usual promises of 'good' and 'bright' cricket were given an airing. In a whimsical editorial, the *Johannesburg Star* suggested that the Australians should be so praised and applauded and swamped with hospitality that they wouldn't 'have the heart to appeal'.

Practice in one net only was available on the Monday and was more of a 'loosener' than serious practice. At the end of an Australian winter and following a long sea voyage, nobody was anxious to risk injury at the start of the tour but the overall impression was favourable, Arthur Morris gaining approval for the ease and style of his strokeplay. Bob Crisp, former South African pace bowler, spoke highly of Morris and gave Neil Harvey the accolade of being 'the most spectacular fieldsman I have ever seen'. This was accurate enough and in stark contrast to Crisp's remark in the same article that Harvey was 'uncomfortable against good spin bowling'. In fact, Harvey was one of the most effective players of spin bowling we've had in Australia. Len Hutton, writing in the *Rand Daily Mail*, considered that in Arthur Morris, Australia had 'another Clem Hill'.

The opening match against Zululand had little joy for Morris who was leg before for 10. Moroney also failed but the middle order, Loxton, Archer, McCool and Ian Johnson, lifted the score to a respectable 8–401 when Hassett declared the innings closed. The locals could only muster 52 and 69, Ian Johnson taking 7 wickets for the match.

Arthur, who was off-colour, failed again in the first innings of the Natal game, falling to the tearaway fast bowler, Cuan McCarthy, for 10. He made amends in the second innings with 153. He and Moroney were severe on all bowlers but McCarthy in particular, had 85 runs taken from his 15 overs. Morris, one report stated: 'lived up to his reputation with late, powerful strokes of all kinds'. Nourse, with 104 not out in Natal's second innings, held the Australians to a draw.

Bill Johnston had been injured in a car accident and was in hospital in Durban. Ironically, the selectors back in Australia were now obliged to ask the discarded Keith Miller if he would be available to make up the numbers in South Africa until Bill Johnston was able to resume, if indeed he was. Miller, after some delay, graciously and without rancour accepted the invitation and was soon on his way, it being hoped he'd be available for the first Test Match.

Morris was out for 29 in the Benoni match against North Transvaal where there was some criticism of the number of bumpers bowled by Lindwall and Walker. The *Rand Daily Mail* was moved to print a short paragraph which may or may not be apocryphal but which indicates clearly the concern which the Australian pace bowlers had caused in post-war games. Washbrook, says the item, was asked by a reporter who were the two best batsmen in the world. 'Me and Len 'Utton' he said. The journalist, a little nonplussed asked, 'What about Bradman and Hassett and Morris?' 'Ah', replied Washbrook, 'they have only to face English bowling. Me and Len have to play Aussie bowling.' The bumper question has been a hardy perennial in cricket circles and is, of course, always high on the list of topics raised when cricket is discussed.

At Bulawayo against Southern Rhodesia, Arthur, with Moroney, gave the side a good start, each making 104 in considerable haste against an ordinary attack, and Australia won easily. Ian Johnson and Colin McCool took 15 of the 20 wickets which fell. Bill Johnston had rejoined the team but was unlikely to play for a further six weeks.

At Salisbury (now Harare) against 'a South African XI', the Australians encountered some high-class off spin bowling from Hugh Tayfield plus some genuine pace from the promising Michael Melle. Morris was out for 43, caught off another off spinner, Jack Waddington. The young Springbok side couldn't cope with the speed and accuracy of Lindwall and Walker and were out for 84 and 156, Lindwall having 7–22 in the match, which was won by an innings. At this point in the tour Morris's average was 70, just below Hassett's 74.

Moving on to Bloemfontein, the tourists came up against the Orange Free State. Morris opened with his captain, Ken Archer coming in at No 3. Arthur was run out for 33 while in full flight and Hassett was only 4 runs short of a century before lunch. Harvey put all bowlers on the rack to be still in occupation at 145 when Hassett mercifully ended the agony for the home team at 3–405. The bowlers tidied the opposition up for 135 and 131 to register another innings win. Arthur Mailey opined that the Australians 'lacked virility' in this game—a surprising conclusion.

Morris had two short stays at the crease in the match against Western Province but the Australians were never in any danger of defeat in the drawn game. The South Africans were finding Lindwall more than a handful and the impending arrival of Keith Miller did not encourage players or critics to optimism for the future. It was mooted too that Bill Johnston might soon be available so that the fire power in view was discouraging.

Miller duly arrived on 4 December and both he and Johnston practised at the Newlands nets. The latter was placed on 'light duties' for a week but his and Miller's early addition to the side gave it more than a nominal lift.

In a two-day non-first-class game against Western Province Country Districts, Morris scored an almost disdainful 146. His century came before lunch with 100 runs in boundaries. Miller had some useful batting practice with 49 and put his arm over briefly in the Country's first innings.

At this stage, Hassett took to his bed with tonsilitis which forced him to miss the match against the formidable Transvaal side which boasted internationals Eric and Athol Rowan, Bruce Mitchell and Michael Melle. Before this game Morris had dropped to No 5 in the averages with 410 runs at 51.25—behind Hassett, Moroney, Loxton and Harvey. Morris struck a lean patch hereabouts and was out in the Transvaal match, in which he captained the side, for 15 and 12. Indeed, the Australians performed poorly on a damp wicket and were out for 84. Athol Rowan, a tall off spinner with a shambling run due to an injury received in the war, had the astonishing figures of 9–19 in the first innings. The home team did little better with 9–125 (declared) and, going in again, the Australians were once again routed. Rowan took 6–49 to give him 15 for 68 in the match, a performance that would take some beating. However, the Australians lifted themselves, and their own off spinner, Ian Johnson, took 6–22 to send the locals packing for 53, five players recording the minimum. Walker and Miller were unable to bowl in the second innings which made the performances of Johnson and Noblet all the more notable. Morris supported his bowlers throughout with attacking fields.

As a Test warm-up the Australians were given a match against a South African eleven at Durban. The home side included a hard core of seasoned players in Eric Rowan, Jack Cheetham and Owen Wynne, plus some promising youngsters who were apparently on the verge of Test selection. Morris was rested with Hassett's return. Jack Moroney and Harvey scored heavily in a rain-affected drawn match.

The Johannesburg Test saw Morris out for 0, caught from a mishit hook at short fine leg from the bowling of McCarthy. However, after losing three quick wickets, the convalescing Hassett played a good captain's knock and, with Sam Loxton, lifted the Australians to a respectable 413 (Hassett 112, Loxton 101). This was more than enough to win. Johnston and Miller shared the bowling honours and Eric Rowan's first innings 60 was top score for the South Africans.

Morris had slipped further down the list in the batting averages and, (excluding the newly arrived Miller) was now lowest of the recognised batsmen with 39.72. Ian Johnson had 50 wickets at 12.5 and was far ahead of the other bowlers. Percy Beames, a Victorian State cricketer, writing in the *Star* expressed disappointment with Morris's loss of form which he attributed to a falling off in concentration. But there was a good distance still to be covered. The South Africans had had the worst of the luck with the weather, and in their second innings had to contend with some unpleasant bite and turn. Despite this Dudley Nourse, Cheetham and John Nel all played exceedingly well. Indeed the selectors considered that the entire eleven had performed well enough to go, unchanged, into the second Test at Newlands, Cape Town. Winning the toss, the Australians left no doubts as to their superiority with a total of 7–526 (declared). Morris scored 42 in good style despite being missed when wicket-keeper Wade fumbled the ball and missed a stumping, with the batsman well out of his ground trying to drive 'Tufty' Mann. This was not a costly miss, as Morris fell 10 runs later flicking at Tayfield to be picked up at slip. The Springboks could only muster 278 despite some good batting by Nourse and the talkative Eric Rowan, a batsman who believed in keeping anyone in close enough proximity informed on the run of play. Arthur Mailey was critical of Lindwall and considered, on his display in this innings, that he might be dropped for the following Test. This may have stirred up the great bowler a little and he replied with 5–32 off 15 overs in the second innings of 333. Dudley Nourse had a great match with 65 and 114 and confirmed, at the age of nearly 40, his place among the world's leading batsmen. This was Nourse's eighth Test century and equalled Bruce Mitchell's tally. The Australians, batting again, lost both Morris (24) and Moroney (19) while reaching the 87 required to win. Harvey's great first innings century had the critics bracketing him with Clem Hill and Frank Woolley.

After two Tests, Arthur Morris, at 22, was third from the bottom of the averages of the recognised batsmen, which were dominated by Neil Harvey with a Bradman-like 117.5. Hassett was, as ever, near the top and his generosity and praise to defeated opponents were much appreciated by his hosts. The same could be said of the genial Manager, 'Chappie' Dwyer.

Morris missed the Eastern Province game at Port Elizabeth which the Australians won comfortably, Keith Miller hitting a spectacular 131, with six sixes. There were rumblings about the number of bumpers bowled by the Australians and urgings for the Test umpires to invoke Law 46(4) regarding the persistent bowling of short pitched deliveries. This objection stood the test of time pretty well but without any visible success until restricted bumpers per over laws were introduced. There were also urgings for the recall of Bruce Mitchell to stiffen the batting.

Moving on to East London for the match against Border, the Australians were, as usual, warmly welcomed. However the universal expressions of goodwill might have faded a little as the visitors ran up 425 runs in 6½ hours. Morris returned to form with a virtuoso display which produced 106 runs with eleven fours. Hassett scored another century, and all the others who batted performed in sparkling fashion. Noblet, Bill Johnston and McCool shared the bowling honours in Border's two lamentable efforts of 72 and 60. Lindwall was used only sparingly and was obviously being saved for the Test match. Back in Australia, Stan McCabe's wife, Edna, had just given birth to a daughter, Christine. The news was received with enthusiasm by the tourists who drank the baby's health during the lunch break at East London.

The selectors were unmoved by the calls to restore Bruce Mitchell to the South African side for the Durban Test and the players who had been heavily defeated in the first two games were retained. Batting first, the Springboks recorded their best first innings effort to date with 311, of which Eric Rowan made a talkative 143 and Nourse 66. The Australians' vulnerability on wet pitches was starkly evident as they collapsed for 75, Hugh Tayfield taking 7–23 from 8.4 overs. An unusual request came from Cuan McCarthy on this occasion when he sought Morris's advice as to what length he should aim for on the damp pitch. Arthur was as non committal as courtesy would permit. Morris top scored with 25 and the only others to reach double figures were Moroney 10 and Sam Loxton 16. Nourse, however, decided to bat again, fearing that the newly laid pitch would prove troublesome when it dried out. The tactic was unsuccessful, the home side being out for 99. Ian Johnson and the ever useful Bill Johnston shared the wickets. This left Australia 336 runs to win in a day and a half on a crumbling wicket. After losing three wickets for 59, Morris and Harvey were not out overnight at 3–80. Morris didn't last long, treading on his wicket for 44, a rare event which distressed him. Neil Harvey, who was becoming a thorough pain in the neck to the South Africans, made a magnificent 151 to be not out when the runs were knocked off for the loss of five wickets. Harvey's Test average from five innings with two not outs was 129.33, Morris's 27. Bill Johnston had 19 Test wickets at 15.89; his place among our great bowlers, though not adequately recognised, is high.

In the return match against the Transvaal, Bruce Mitchell did little to advance his prospects of a recall to his country's side, being out for 7 and 15, the blistering pace of Miller and Walker being too much for him. After the home side was bowled out for 122, Arthur Morris, on a lively wicket, guided his side to a moderate but sufficient 223 (Morris 103). It must be stated that Arthur was actively assisted in this innings by some slipshod catching. A young medium-pacer, Guido Keightley-Smith, took 6–66, moving the ball both ways off a grassy pitch. Transvaal's second innings of 161 forced the Australians to bat again, Morris being not out 33 when the 61 runs needed were knocked off. There was still some anger at the number of bumpers bowled, with local scribes joining R S Whitington (an Australian) in deploring them. What will we do when there aren't any fast bowlers around to fan this argument? On this occasion Morris was rebuked for allowing the overdose of short balls to continue, although he always discouraged this type of delivery against tail end batsmen.

Arthur Morris was carrying out his duties as vice-captain, both on and off the field in a manner that one would expect. A picture in the *Johannesburg Star* shows him in an official capacity with the Australian High Commissioner at a function to mark the 162nd anniversary of the first British settlement in Australia in 1788.

The South African selectors took the chopper to the side for the fourth Test, with five previous players making an unceremonious exit—Wynne, Watkins, Smith, Wade and Cheetham making way for Denis Begbie, Ron Draper, Michael Melle, George Fullerton and Paul Winslow. All but Draper the wicket-keeper were from the Transvaal.

In a training run against a country side at Witbank in the North East of the Transvaal, the Australians scored 8–338 and dismissed the home team twice for 73 and 100. Morris made 30 and Bill Johnston was among the wickets again.

The Australians again scored heavily in the Test, batting first at Ellis Park, Johannesburg. Openers Morris and Moroney both scored centuries in an opening partnership of 214 which was described as 'drab' by a local scribe. Miller livened things up on the second day but it took till nearly tea time for the Australians to complete their innings with 8 wickets down. Young Melle had a splendid introduction to Test cricket with 5–113, and both he and McCarthy gave the Australians some of their own back with a leavening of bumpers, one of which removed Keith Miller's cap. Arthur considered Melle a very good fast-medium bowler. Miller no doubt registered this incident in the 'untearable note-book' (the mind) for future reference. The home team started brightly, Eric Rowan again being in the runs with 55. Sadly, those that followed saw the side slump from 1–84 to 6–148 before the tail wagged vigor-ously to raise the total to a respectable 352. Hassett had to use eight bowlers, Lindwall taking 3–82 and Miller 3–75. Morris was out for 19 in the Australian second innings, in which Harvey again scored heavily. Moroney's second century of the match earned him few friends in the visitors' 2–259. Neil Harvey's great Test run was continuing with 544 runs at 136. Morris was still nearer the bottom than the top with 265 runs at 37.9. The South Africans earned an honourable draw in this game.

The tour was now entering the home run as the Australians made for Kimberley to play Griqualand West, pondering a little perhaps on the hostile criticism levelled both locally and at home of what was seen as 'negative cricket' in the fourth Test. Morris scored 50 and 102 not out in the Kimberley game, which was drawn after some bright batting. Harvey passed Jack Fingleton's aggregate of 1192 runs made in the 1935–36 tour, when he flayed the hapless Griqualanders for his seventh tour century, batting with an equally aggressive Morris. The latter's 102 was his sixth century of the tour.

At Ladysmith, a name redolent of the Boer War and General Roberts, the Australians were bowled out for 74 on a damp wicket but recovered sufficiently in their second innings to win comfortably against a Natal Country side. Morris made 9 and 44 in a low scoring match.

There was a rumpus at the withdrawal by Dick Ashdown from the umpires' Test panel following what he deemed to be a reprimand by J P W Howden, president of the South African Cricket Association, for some 'doubtful' decisions way back in the first Test. No Australian was involved.

Morris missed the return game against Natal at Pietermaritzberg. The Tayfield brothers, Hugh and Arthur, both off spinners, took 9 wickets between them in the Australian first innings. The game was drawn.

The final Test at Port Elizabeth produced an early surprise when Ray Lindwall was replaced by Noblet. Arthur Morris had the unpopular duty of acquainting Lindwall of this selection bombshell and recalls that the fast bowler was less than impressed. To the end of the fourth Test, Lindwall, with 12 wickets at 20.7 was second to Bill Johnston, 20 at 18.5, so the decision was, on the face of it, far from easy to explain to an indignant Lindwall.

The final game was virtually decided when the Australians scored 7–549 after winning the toss, despite the early dismissal of Moroney and Miller. Morris and Harvey came together, with Harvey doing more of the attacking while Arthur played his best innings of the tour, calmly garnering runs with measured strokes to all points in a classical opener's display. Harvey was out at 236 and Morris for 157 at 350 after 315 minutes. Hassett went on to 167 the following day to guide his side to a winning total. Miller and Noblet then ripped through the early South African batting and the hapless Springboks were again facing a crushing defeat at 7–104 at the end of the second day. Nourse and Rowan offered some resistance, and later 'Tufty' Mann, batting at No 10, restored some dignity to the side with a hurricane 41 in 36 minutes with two sixes and four fours. The innings ended at 158.

Following on, the locals crumbled completely for 132, Nourse a solitary defiant bastion in a batting catastrophe. His 55 brought his runs scored to 405 at 45 and pushed him fractionally ahead of Eric Rowan's 404 at 44.89. The other recognised batsmen were nowhere. Among the Australians, Harvey's figures were Bradman-like—660 runs at 132.

Morris lifted himself into third spot, behind Lindsay Hassett, with 422 runs at 52.75. Bill Johnston was best of the regular bowlers with 23 wickets at 17.04. All the regular bowlers did well. Miller's arrival was a very significant contribution in both the batting and bowling areas, confirming his position as the world's best all-rounder.

The final result of four wins to Australia and one drawn game was an accurate reflection of the relative performances of the two sides. Despite the generous remarks of Lindsay Hassett and Chappie Dwyer, the Australians were vastly superior in all departments and the South African press had some scathing criticisms of their team's showing, particularly in the final Test.

Little remained but to wind up the tour and head homewards. Arthur scored a classy 103 against Western Province and joined Harvey in a final tally of eight centuries for the tour, equalling Denis Compton's total a year before. Arthur's strong finish raised him in the first-class tour averages to third spot. Harvey had scored a fantastic 1526 runs at 76.30, Hassett 889 and 68.38, Morris 1411 at 58.79.

He had demonstrated again his pre-eminence among opening batsmen of the world and, after a patchy middle period, he'd shown an ability to claw his way back to a significant and indispensable position in his team. Arthur and several others stayed behind to visit the game reserve and other scenic spots before returning home.

Chappie Dwyer and Lindsay Hassett both expressed appreciation of the manner in which the tour had been handled and of the hospitality received and goodwill enjoyed. The side was unbeaten and had scarcely ever looked like being beaten, despite some uneasiness on damp or drying wickets—a well known and perennial Australian phenomenon. Chappie Dwyer paid special tribute to Dudley Nourse, naming him 'one of the world's greatest cricketers today'. Hassett endorsed this, adding that Nourse was a 'grand fellow both on and off the field'.

For Arthur Morris, the tour has many treasured memories. On the cricket field he had confirmed his position as one of the world's great batsmen. At the same time he had impressed his colleagues, opponents and the public generally that he was a man who complemented the manager and captain perfectly by his behaviour on and off the field.

Like most Australians who toured there, the South African experience rates at the top of his cricket memories, both in terms of the cricket played and the hospitality enjoyed. The Australians who visited South Africa more than a decade before expressed similar sentiments.

England

Turns the Corner

AUSTRALIA

1950–51

'Lettuces with hearts as big, as
Freddie Brown's!'—Sydney barrowman

ON THE TEAM'S RETURN HOME, Arthur Morris journeyed by ship all the way to Sydney while some players took planes for the last leg of the trip from Perth to the Eastern States. Keith Miller and Ian Johnson undertook some writing engagements for the *Johannesburg Sunday Times* and *Sunday Express* respectively. The question of bumpers was inevitably to the fore. Miller pointed to a valid contrast between the bumper as bowled by him and Lindwall and that used by Larwood and Voce in 1932–33 when the attack was rendered lethal by a packed leg side field. Miller also considered it 'a calamity' that Bruce Mitchell had been excluded from the South African sides. Chappie Dwyer, in the *Rand Daily Mail*, was critical of the penchant for half-cocked forward prodding so prevalent in South Africa and urged the Springboks to profit from the batting of Morris, Harvey and Hassett as skilful exponents of back foot play. There had certainly been plenty of opportunity to observe these three in the tour just concluded.

Arthur Morris took up the pen also in an article in *Spotlight*, a South African weekly paper. He made the point that English-style coaching had been detrimental to young players and emphasised the need to get on to the back foot unless the ball could be driven. Arthur considered, too, that 'provincialism', which could be roughly equated to 'interstate rivalry', in Australia had been detrimental to selections. He defended the use of the bumper as a legitimate 'surprise ball' but was critical of McCarthy who, when he finally decided to use such a delivery, used it so frequently that the surprise element was missing.

All sorts of people were picking their 'world teams' and Arthur Morris was favoured unanimously to partner Len Hutton in opening the innings. It wasn't so easy to pick the other nine and there was some radically different thinking, particularly in the bowling area.

Whilst on tour in South Africa, Arthur had received a cabled invitation from the New South Wales Liberal Party inviting him to stand as a candidate for the forthcoming State elections. Morris declined with thanks adding wryly: 'Fancy me, as a Liberal representative, fielding in front of all the Labor boys near the Sydney 'Hill' and misfielding a ball. Life would hardly be worth living.'

The winter lay-off following the cricketers' return from South Africa enabled them and the public to speculate on the forthcoming tour of Australia by the MCC in search of the Ashes so convincingly won by Australia in 1946–47 and 1948. Although England had won in South Africa in the 1948–49 season, there was little evidence that they'd be strong enough to defeat Australia at home. However the coming series between the two oldest cricketing countries was to be the first for many years in which the towering (figuratively speaking) and all-pervasive figure of D G Bradman would be missing—a fact that must have been heartening to the people at Lord's.

For Arthur Morris, the season proved to be a mixed one. He scored heavily in State games but had to wait until the fourth Test for success at the top level. The England side was a strange mixture of experience and untried youth. The moguls at Lord's were predictably reluctant (or not yet ready) to appoint a professional to lead the team and went through the process of inviting F G Mann of Middlesex and Norman Yardley of Yorkshire (both of whom declined) before settling on F R Brown of Northampton as captain. 'Freddie' Brown had last visited Australia as a 'supernumerary' in Jardine's side of 1932–33. He was a fairly run-of-the-mill slow-medium leg spinner whose quality was not tested out here in 1932 but who, on the rare occasions when he was on view, showed that he was certainly no Bill O'Reilly. As things turned out in 1950, the choice of Brown was a singularly happy and fruitful one. He was a genial, forthright, ruddy faced Englishman to whom Australians quickly related and warmed. As captain, he was innovative and aggressive and in both batting and bowling performed far better than anyone anticipated. The MCC unbent enough to give him Denis Compton as vice-captain.

The others chosen were:

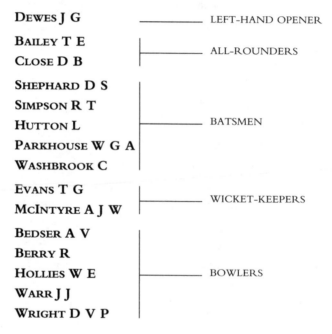

Dewes J G	LEFT-HAND OPENER
Bailey T E **Close D B**	ALL-ROUNDERS
Shephard D S **Simpson R T** **Hutton L** **Parkhouse W G A** **Washbrook C**	BATSMEN
Evans T G **McIntyre A J W**	WICKET-KEEPERS
Bedser A V **Berry R** **Hollies W E** **Warr J J** **Wright D V P**	BOWLERS

There were no doubts as to the quality of Hutton, Washbrook and Compton as batsmen, nor of Bedser and Wright as bowlers. The pace department was scantily served by Warr and Bailey as supporters for Alec Bedser. None of the three was above fast-medium and they were unlikely, apart from Bedser, to trouble the best batsmen. Dewes, Sheppard, Parkhouse and Simpson were unknown quantities with the bat but much was hoped for from the youngest member, Brian Close, a 19-year-old from Yorkshire. Close was, in the event, disappointing.

To everyone's surprise this team, on paper quite unconvincing, did far better than the players or anyone else expected. Hutton batted superbly throughout as he was bound to do one day, Washbrook, Parkhouse and Simpson performed well on occasion, and the bowlers excelled themselves, Bedser, Bailey and Brown performing prodigies of tireless energy and application. It's fair to say that if Compton had performed near to his best, England may have gone close to winning the series. Compton's failure was almost unbelievable—8 Test innings for 53 runs with a top score of 23. The only reward the capricious game of cricket had to offer Compton was to allow him to be there 'at the death' when Len Hutton hit the winning run in the fifth Test match to give England its first post-war victory against Australia by eight wickets.

Edrich's omission was regretted and before the side embarked, Jack Hobbs and Frank Woolley were both pessimistic, Hobbs predicting 'a towsing' and Woolley bemoaning England's loss of the 'urge to attack'.

Morris had started in convincing form with scores of 74, 101 and 78 not out in two games against Queensland, and followed with a rousing 168 against the Englishmen, who'd been meandering around the continent with moderate success, but generating a lot of goodwill. Indeed, Australian crowds were so taken with Freddie Brown and his men that one heard on all sides the unusual hope voiced that 'the Poms would win'.

In the New South Wales game, Morris and Miller added 265 for the second wicket. Bill O'Reilly in the *Sydney Morning Herald* remarked on Morris's 'uncanny ability to get the ball away with scoring shots on the on-side', and added that his 'timing and placing left nothing to be desired'. The MCC bowling figures were far from impressive—Bedser 1–127, Wright 0–93, Hollies 1–138. Morris batted for just on four hours and hit one six and eighteen fours in his 168. Hutton and Compton both scored heavily but the others, apart from Washbrook (50 and 53 not out), were disappointing. The game was drawn.

In two Shield matches against South Australia and Victoria, Arthur had only moderate success, and in the Brisbane Test he fell twice to Bedser, lbw for 25 and caught by Bailey for 0. In an exciting, rain-affected match, with uncovered wickets and Brisbane's erratic summer weather, Australia finally won by 70 runs despite a masterly second innings of 62 not out by Hutton, who finally ran out of partners chasing 193. Bedser and Bailey both had seven wickets for the match and Australia's 'mystery' bowler, Jack Iverson, took 4–43 in England's second innings.

Morris scored an even century for an Australian eleven against the MCC in Sydney, before making a gift of his wicket to Lancashire left-hander, Bob Berry, who'd had little joy so far on tour. He'd taken 166 minutes to reach three figures and unselfishly made way for younger players, Burke and Hole, to get some top-class practice. Compton scored 115, not in his best style but full of character and determination and giving hope of better things to come.

The second Test played in Melbourne was again a low scoring match, won by Australia by 28 runs. Morris failed twice with 2 and 18; indeed both sides batted unconvincingly. In the first innings, Bedser had him caught by Hutton at slip switching his line of attack from leg stump to off stump and luring Arthur to attempt a drive from a ball moving away. In the second innings, Wright had him leg before, not playing a stroke and allowing a straight ball to hit his pads. Morris thought Wright a great bowler with lots of bounce and top spin. He says, 'I never played against a bowler who beat batsmen, including me, so often'. The pronounced 'bounce' often resulted in excellent deliveries going over the top of the stumps.

Arthur found him a 'delightful opponent' and once after he'd been hit for six from a no-ball, told Arthur he didn't mind his no-balls being hit for four but not six! Frequent no-balls and one or two loose deliveries per over took some of the pressure off the batsman. Compton was unfit and when England dropped Hutton down the batting order, the scribes and many others scratched their heads. If you have the world's finest opener, why bat him at No 4? Bedser bowled beautifully and, at this stage, had trapped Morris three times out of their last four encounters. Iverson was proving a problem to the Englishmen with his freakish spinners, flicked like a marble from a large hand, with little indication as to whether the ball would come from off or leg or go straight on. Australia's batting failures in four innings were provoking much argument up and down the land and there was general approval and appreciation for the manner

England, under Freddie Brown, was approaching a task popularly believed a short time before to be beyond them.

Morris was back in the runs at Sydney in the return match against the MCC—a prelude to the third Test. Rain interrupted the game, but Morris (105) and Miller (98) scored heavily against an attack weakened by Bedser's omission. The punishment meted out by the pair in a stand of 140, plus an injury to Warr, forced Brown into an uncharacteristic role with a very deep-set field which limited boundaries but made easy the taking of singles from nearly every ball. Apart from Jim de Courcy, no other New South Wales batsman troubled the bowlers and the total of 333 was modest enough after the whirlwind opening. Morris had a patchy start in this innings but blossomed as it progressed, with Wright and Hollies expensive.

The tourists lost Washbrook and Sheppard early but then Hutton and Simpson came together and added 236 for the third wicket in just over even time. 'Hutton played beautifully', said Jim Swanton, 'with the sense of untroubled mastery that no modern batsman conveys to the same degree'. He batted for 253 minutes and was untroubled by the quota of bumpers dished out by Lindwall, Miller and Walker. Simpson's 259 provided him with good practice and was heartening for his colleagues. An elegant player, he reminded some of Joe Hardstaff Junior, his teammate in the Nottingham side. The match petered out due to rain interruptions after Morris had hit his wicket when facing Brown with his second innings score at 14.

The Sydney Test was a particularly disappointing affair after the two previous performances. Batting first, with Compton back in the side, England supporters had reason to feel that this match might see them end the post-war drought. The weather was fine, the wicket beyond reproach, but the batting, apart from Hutton, Brown and Washbrook, was fragile. After Hutton and Simpson had added 94 for the second wicket, Miller fragmented the innings by despatching both Simpson and Compton in one over, and had Hutton (who had looked immovable other than by some violent natural disturbance) leg before nine runs later. Parkhouse got 26 but Freddie Brown, bulky and brick red of face, put some stiffening into the innings, applying the bat's full face to the ball in some splendid straight and off driving. Iverson went wicketless in England's first innings but his time was coming. England's 290 took until mid-afternoon on the second day, and when Australia batted, Morris was bowled by Bedser for 0. The big man coaxed Arthur across the wicket and hit the exposed leg stump. This was Bedser's fourth Morris scalp in the five encounters to date. Keith Miller and Hassett played some effective, if uninteresting, cricket and with support from Archer and Ian Johnson, Australia finished with 426. In a marathon, if funereal bowling effort, Bedser, Warr and Brown carried the England attack in the absence of an injured Trevor Bailey and Doug Wright. In hot, humid conditions, the trio sent down 123 overs, the only other bowler being Compton who provided a brief six over spell. The England second innings was a disaster. On a wicket taking a little spin, Iverson reduced the cream of England's batsmen to puerile ineffectiveness. Iverson had the extraordinary figures of 19.4 overs, 8 maidens, 6 for 27, the six being the first four batsmen plus Brown and Bedser. Compton scored 23 by guess and by God and it was sad to see so great a player in such a plight. Australia had a resounding innings win.

Jack Iverson shot across the cricketing scene and was gone after two seasons. Arthur recalls that he possessed very large hands and flicked the ball out with his middle finger. This made it difficult to judge which way it would spin. 'As I always picked the bowler's spin from the hand' Arthur recalls, 'I had a lot of difficulty with him although I scored a century against him in an interstate game'. Arthur thinks he would have been 'a sensation' had he gone to England in the 1953 team. 'I think he expected to have success every time he bowled and, not having been subjected to the toil and sweat that other bowlers endure because of his late entry into the game, he quit early' concludes Morris. Arthur might have added that the hiding handed out to him in a Shield match by himself and Keith Miller probably hastened his early retirement.

Morris had yet to get the breaks in a Test innings but there was little wrong with his form, some said, as long as Bedser wasn't in the opposition, an unkind observation soon to be emphatically disproved. Before going on to Adelaide for the fourth Test, Arthur plundered the Victorian attack to the tune of 182 at the Sydney Cricket Ground. This put him in a positive frame of mind for the Adelaide match, in which he had something to prove. On a good Adelaide wicket, Morris batted down the long, sundrenched day to be 140 not out, of a total of 3–254. Swanton described his innings as 'competent, watchful, phlegmatic with hardly a hint of mortal error'. Jack Fingleton was a little more exuberant and wrote that the occasion was a 'red-letter day' for Morris, during which he laid to rest the nagging and ragging he'd been receiving about 'the Bedser hoodoo'. He played Bedser with style and confidence to be 206 before being bowled, a victim of weariness, by Roy Tattersall, a reserve off spinner flown from England to bolster the injury-plagued England attack. Morris's resurgence, immensely satisfying to him, was timely, for the remaining ten batsmen could only muster 165 between them, including sundries. In this his seventh century innings against England, he overtook two better-than-average performers in Victor Trumper and Bill Woodfull and was now second only to Bradman, far ahead with 19. England should have been well in this match with good batting conditions and facing a moderate total for the Adelaide Oval. They faltered badly with the honourable exception of Hutton, who provided, said Jim Swanton, 'batsmanship that was the nearest possible approach to perfection'. This was fair comment despite a bad stumping miss by Tallon from Ian Johnson's bowling. Hutton carried his bat for 156, the first Englishman to do so against Australia since Bobby Abel in Sydney in 1892. England's total of 272 looked to be exceedingly vulnerable.

On the subject of openers 'carrying their bat', Morris is an unbeliever. He contends that if an opener survives until the last man joins him, he, the opener, should throw the bat at anything he can reach in an effort to add runs, something No 11 batsmen don't usually manage to do. If the batsman gets out, too bad. In other words, 'carrying your bat' is something of an ego trip. Bill Woodfull, who did it twice, might not have agreed.

In the second innings Arthur Morris was run out for 16 answering an impossible call from his opening partner, Ken Archer. The Australians made 403 for 8 wickets in their second innings, giving England something over 500 to win—a task beyond many better sides than this present one. They were short 274 runs, giving Australia their fourth win of the season. The home side did not even need the indisposed Iverson to see England off for 228.

Before the final Test was played in Melbourne, Morris had a Sheffield Shield match to play against South Australia in Sydney. He was run out for 8, the second run out in successive innings. Meanwhile the MCC took on Victoria in the return game at the Melbourne Cricket Ground. The match was drawn, but was notable because of a double century by Lindsay Hassett who shed the cares of Test captaincy and played in his 'Saturday afternoon' fashion, his 232 coming up in six hours. Trevor Bailey also made a century, one presumes in fairly sedate style, but the match ended in an unnecessary draw which didn't gain cricket many friends.

There were doubts about Brown's fitness for the final Test, but his strained thigh muscle stood up to a searching test on the eve of the game and he led the side on what proved an historic occasion. Bailey came back for Warr who, apart from having a big heart and a sense of humour, was scarcely Test class. Graeme Hole came into the Australian side in place of Archer, and Hassett won the toss again. Jack Fingleton commented that Morris 'probably covers more ground playing a defensive stroke than any other batsman of note'. This is probably a reference to the 'shuffle' Arthur had developed. On the other hand it may rather have been that he used the full distance between stumps and batting crease when playing back. For Morris to take just on three hours to score 50 runs was completely out of character and it was obvious that he was not in good touch. Frustrated, he had a dip at Brown and was leg before without adding to his half century. Hassett made 92 runs of varying quality but the side was out for 217, Bedser and Brown taking five wickets each and bowling 40 of the 69 overs completed in the innings.

This was surely England's chance, but a day lost to rain didn't help their cause. Hutton batted in his grandest manner but with some well deserved luck. His batting on the tour brought to mind the classical play of England's greatest batsman, Jack Hobbs. Simpson was again in good form but his side just passed Australia's total at stumps on day three, with six wickets down and Bedser batting with Simpson. The partnership flourished next day with Simpson taking the long handle to all bowlers to be 156 not out when the England innings closed at 320. He'd batted 5½ hours in a display of great merit despite some dull periods.

When Australia batted again, Morris was soon out leg before trying to swing Bedser to leg from a delivery which, he seemed to think, had pitched outside leg stump. He has an open mind on the matter now. The others, apart from Hassett, Hole and Harvey, surrendered rather limply and the side was out for 197. England knocked off the 90-odd runs with the loss of Washbrook and Simpson, to win by 8 wickets. Hutton was there at the close with 60 and with him was Denis Compton. One hoped that being there at the end was some compensation to Compton for an inexplicably poor run in the Test matches.

The England victory was lustily cheered by the crowd who felt that, apart from anything else, Brown, Hutton and Bedser had earned a victory following their lion-hearted efforts throughout the summer.

Hutton averaged 88.8 in the Tests, more than double the next contender. Bedser, in a display reminiscent of Maurice Tate in his great days, took 30 Australian wickets at 16, and Brown 18 at 21.6.

Arthur Morris had a patchy Test series, lifted to respectability by his Adelaide double century. He was fifth in the Test match batting averages with 321 runs at 35.6, and many were wondering if Bedser did indeed have his measure. Over the entire domestic season, his form had been well up to his usual high standard with 1221 runs at 58.14, including six centuries and three fifties, a fairly high strike rate for an opening batsman.

Ray Robinson, writing in the *Sydney Sun* before the Adelaide Test, dealt in some detail with the 'hoodoo' the 'Lion of Surrey' held not only for Morris. He pointed out that Bradman had fallen frequently to Bedser, notably in England in 1948 when Don several times steered the late inswinger into the hands of leg gully. Robinson questioned the sideways shuffle in Morris's batting which had become evident during the summer. He concluded that Arthur was on the move as he played at the ball so that, apart from exposing his leg stump, Bedser's late outswinger was finding the bat's edge with a resultant catch for slip. A photo of one dismissal shows Morris at the end of his stroke almost a yard wide of the stumps on the off side as the ball flies waist high to Hutton at slip. Robinson concluded that it would be premature to write Morris off as Bedser's 'bunny' and indeed, even if Alec took Arthur's wicket 22 times in their 48 encounters, it can be fairly argued that an opening batsman is more likely than others to fall to an opening bowler. More than that, Bedser paid dearly for many of his successes and Arthur's batting average in these encounters was 61.11. There were many prolific days ahead for Arthur Morris and Alec Bedser.

The season just concluded marked a turning point in England's cricketing fortunes and the 1953, 1954–55 and 1956 engagements were to see them again lording it over their Antipodean cousins.

Two Home Series —WEST INDIES and SOUTH AFRICA

Arthur meets 'The Three W's'

THE WEST INDIES HAD SENT NO TEAM to Australia since 1931–32 when they took one Test from Australia despite the presence of players like Bradman, Ponsford, Woodfull, McCabe, and Grimmett. The star players were George Headley with the bat and Learie Constantine, a spectacular all-round cricketer of staggering ability. He was a tremendous hitter, a fast bowler of quality and the most acrobatic and versatile fieldsman of his time. George Headley had earned the sobriquet of the 'Black Bradman' following his capable handling of Grimmett and his Test career spanned almost two decades. Like most of the great batsmen of the past 60 years, he was predominantly a back-foot player, although his driving was spectacular when the ball could be reached on the forward stroke. He topped 1000 runs on this Australian tour, scored two Test centuries and carried the batting of a beaten side on his shoulders.

A side from the Caribbean was scheduled to visit Australia in the summer of 1951–52 and, following some splendid performances in England in the summer of 1950, their visit was keenly awaited. The 'three W's', Everton Weekes, Frank Worrell and Clyde Walcott, had put the English counties to the sword and performed almost as sensationally in the Tests. In summary, this was their output:

	First-Class Games	Avge	Tests	Avge
Walcott	1674	55.8	229	45.8
Weekes	2310	79.65	338	56.3
Worrell	1775	68.26	539	89.83

In Sonny Ramadhin and Alf Valentine the West Indians had two notable bowlers who were key figures in the series win against England. Ramadhin was indeed a puzzle to the best of players. A small man, who bowled with sleeves buttoned down, his repertoire included off and leg breaks of immaculate length, the direction of spin being hard to pick from the hand. Arthur found him a problem until he could discern the direction of turn. It seems he used finger rather than wrist spin and the speed with which his arm came over at the point of delivery bamboozled the England batsmen. He took 26 Test wickets in 4 matches at 23.23 and 135 wickets at 14.88 on the tour. Valentine, a left-hand slow finger spinner of orthodox methods, was even more successful in the Tests with 33 wickets at 20.42 and 123 at 17.94 for the tour.

The tourists were led by John Goddard, a capable all-rounder. Much interest and speculation abounded as to whether the 'three W's' would reproduce their England form against the genuine speed of Lindwall and Miller and the variety of Bill Johnston. The wiles of Ramadhin and Valentine would be severely tested against players like Morris, Harvey, Hassett and Miller.

The itinerary arranged for the visitors, with only one first-class game before the first Test, put them at a disadvantage. In a low scoring series, the 'three W's' fared far worse than in England. In their defence it should be said that the use of the bumper by Lindwall and Miller was both judicious and frequent, and put Weekes and Walcott, particularly, off their game. The wickets, hard and true, did not provide the 'grip' that Valentine and Ramadhin had enjoyed in England while weaving their magic.

Arthur Morris, still plagued by press comments as to his perceived failure to combat Bedser, had used the winter to do a little self-analysis and soul searching. In an interview he expressed the opinion that he'd been too anxious to play strokes on the leg side, to the detriment of his off side play on which his earlier successes had been founded.

He certainly got away to a promising start in the Sheffield Shield match against Queensland in Brisbane with a rousing 253, the last 50 of which came up in 17 minutes. Morris contributed far more than half his side's total of 400 which was sufficient to gain them a first innings win despite some fine batting by Ken Archer.

The Test against the West Indies followed immediately upon the Brisbane Shield match and provided some interesting and exciting cricket as low scoring games usually do. Lindwall and Miller quickly made it clear that batting against Australians on hard wickets bore no relationship to the gentler encounters the West Indians had experienced in England a few months before. Weekes made a fine 70 in the second innings despite some unwelcome attention by the Australian pace bowlers. The two spinners also performed well, Valentine having 5–99 in Australia's first innings, while the Eastern magic woven by Ramadhin in the second innings took 5 of the 7 wickets that fell for 90 runs. Arthur Morris had a good match double relative to the moderate totals—Valentine had him for 33 in the first innings, Ramadhin for 48 in the second. Arthur maintains that these two were among the best spinners he faced. Lindwall top-scored for Australia in the match with 61, and Doug Ring claimed 6–80 in the visitors' second innings. Australia won the game by 3 wickets but neither side had been really convincing.

Coming to Sydney, the tourists played the State side. Morris was out of luck, falling early to the bowling of Gerry Gomez, a useful middle order batsman and a good mover of the ball at medium pace. Apart from that, he was an agile and almost infallible close-in catcher and his value on this tour can't be overstated.

The Test match which followed hard on the heels of the State game was the only one when scores were anything other than moderate. But Morris did not participate in the run-scoring. In Australia's first innings of 517 he was out for 11, caught behind by Walcott from the bowling of the 34-year-old Prior Jones who bowled fastish and swung the ball a little each way. Hassett and Miller both scored centuries in this innings after the West Indies had been dismissed for 362. In their second innings, the visitors could manage only 290, leaving Australia just 137 to win, a task they accomplished with the loss of only three wickets, including that of Arthur Morris for 30. Morris was out trying to hit Ramadhin off his length, misjudging the flight, missing the ball and being stumped. He was happy to acknowledge a good piece of bowling. Ramadhin was collared in this match by Hassett, Miller and Doug Ring but Valentine, with 4–111, showed his class against some fairly heavy odds. Curiously, both Harvey and Morris were having a lean series so far, but Gomez again demonstrated his value with his second fifty in successive matches.

With Hassett unfit, Arthur Morris was appointed captain for the Adelaide Test. Sid Barnes had been selected to play but was virtually 'vetoed' by the Board of Control 'for reasons other than cricketing ability'. These reasons were never made clear by the Board. Rather sadly, Barnes, a somewhat unusual and unconventional character, never again represented his country. Like Ponsford, he was one of the most difficult of all batsmen to dislodge, with a bat and pads and backside whose size and width appeared to be in flagrant violation of the rules. Morris rates him well ahead of others with whom he opened the innings, except Bill Brown. Barnes and Brown were always ready for the quick single while some were inclined to lean 'on their perches' showing no great inclination to gain or surrender the strike. To this strange edict against Barnes, the Board added injury to insult and forbade the selectors to name another batsman. So Morris's batting strength was reduced by two (Barnes and Hassett) while he had a surfeit of bowlers—Noblet who had been in the twelve chosen coming into the eleven. With Lindwall, Noblet, Bill Johnston, Ian Johnson, Ring and Miller, he had an embarrassment of riches in the bowling department. Arthur was far from happy with the composition of the side. His misgivings proved to be well founded.

In the two Shield matches played prior to the next Test in this curiously arranged season, Morris had an emphatic return to his best form in Melbourne and both he and Barnes scored heavily. Barnes had not yet been banished and he and Arthur Morris added 210 for the first wicket, Barnes being dismissed for 107. Both men notched their centuries in three hours

Morris drives Hollies through the covers at the Oval 5th Test, 1948. Arthur was run out for 196.

Morris on-drives McCool on his way to a century innings against Queensland 1948–49.

Morris with American Baseball star Mickey Mantle, Yankee
Stadium, New York, 1960.

Two older friendly opponents meet 20 years on—Arthur with
Denis Compton, Sydney 1970.

Arthur says a few words about Bill Edrich at the Berkeley
Hotel, London, 1976. This was a special function arranged for
the former England player by Morris's friend, Raphael
Djanogli.

Arthur Morris and Sid Barnes go out to open for Australia—
1st Test, Brisbane, 1946. Neither scored heavily.

Arthur with Sir Donald Bradman at a function in Adelaide in 1984 arranged for captains of all cricketing nations, who had led their sides in an Adelaide Test.

Arthur with first wife Valerie, 1954.

Morris hits to leg.

Arthur with Judith Menmuir, second wife, on the occasion of their marriage, 1968.

Army Rugby side to play City Colts, 1942. Army won 57–0. Morris at five-eighth scored 3 tries. This side contained no fewer than 7 past and future internationals.

and Morris continued to lay about him in an impressive display. In the return game played at Sydney the following week, he was not so successful, scoring 18 and 27, caught behind in both innings from Bill Johnston's bowling as he'd been in the Melbourne innings.

Bill Johnston had now claimed Arthur's wicket three times in succession—once in Melbourne for 210 and later twice in Sydney as mentioned. It would not be fair to say Arthur was in some trepidation facing Johnston, particularly after scoring a double century but he held him in great respect. Unlike Bruce Reid, Johnston's stock ball was the away swinger to Morris but he bowled a beauty that went the other way as well. These three successive dismissals resulted in catches to wicket-keeper, Ian McDonald. Arthur recalls 'they went away very late and found the edge.'

In the Adelaide Test against the West Indies, Morris elected to bat after winning the toss but the move proved disastrous. He was bowled by Frank Worrell, an orthodox slow-medium left-hander, for 1 in a total of 82. Worrell, exploiting a damp patch on the wicket, had 6–38. The visitors did little better and were out for 105 the same day. It was a left-hand bowlers' picnic, Bill Johnston taking 6–62. Arthur performed creditably in the second innings, being second top score with 45 out of 255. Left-hand bowlers were again to the fore, this time Valentine taking the honours with 6–102, including Morris. Needing 233 to win, the Calypso boys proceeded, on Christmas Day on a much improved track, to knock these off for the loss of 4 wickets. This six-wicket victory was an upset result and it may, with some justice, be argued that although the result would have been reversed had Morris elected to field, the Australian batting was proving vulnerable even on reasonable surfaces as in their second innings.

The fourth Test in Melbourne was an exciting match which contained little joy for Morris, who contributed only 6 and 12. He was bowled by John Trim, a fast-medium right-hand bowler in the first innings and was leg before to the consistently effective, bespectacled, Valentine in the second. Ramadhin was not presenting great problems at this stage and seemed to have lost confidence following a couple of maulings in earlier games. The scores were moderate in Melbourne.

Worrell demonstrated his class with a first innings 108, with the reliable Gomez making his usual valuable half century in the second. Hassett and Harvey played well, the latter's 83 being his best for the series. Australia won by 1 wicket after being set 260 to win.

This Adelaide match was Morris's last for the season. Overall he had played in only eight matches for a total of 698 runs from 13 innings at 53.69. Apart from his two Shield double centuries, he did not pass 50. If one takes the two double centuries from his aggregate, the surprising result is that, in 11 other innings, he totalled only 235 runs. I make this point merely to illustrate that the season was far removed from his extraordinary previous consistency. In earlier seasons, he had contributed 50 or more close enough to every second innings. For example:

Season	Innings (Inc NO)	Scores over 50	% To Innings Played
1946–47	20	10	50%
1947–48	16	7	44%
1948 (ENG)	29	14	48%
1949–50 (STH AFRICA)	27	9	33%
1950–51	22	9	41%
1951–52	13	2	15%

In later seasons his consistency was more variable:

Season	Innings (Inc NO)	Scores over 50	% To Innings Played
1952–53	21	8	39%
1953 (ENG)	37	12	32%
1953–54	10	4	40%
1954–55	12	2	17%
1954–55 (WI)	11	4	36%

Overall, Morris played 250 first-class innings for 92 returns of over 50, a percentage of almost 37%, a figure which marks him down as one of the most consistent players of all time. It is almost exactly the same as one of his mentors and heroes, the late Stan McCabe. Stan is generally regarded as a model of consistency, notwithstanding a relative shortfall in centuries—McCabe 29, Morris 46. It need scarcely be said that the incredible Bradman is so far ahead of the others that comparison is particularly odious—55%.

It seems that this 1951–52 season was one in which Morris experienced a slump in his fortunes, but it was certainly premature to assume that his best days were gone forever. There were some great innings still to come.

Reputations suffered in both sides when the accounting for this tour was done. Harvey, who'd averaged 132 in South Africa two seasons before, came back to 26, Morris 53 to 22, while the 'three W's', from whom so much was expected, found the conditions much different and the opposition tougher. Of the three, Arthur considered Weekes the most technically correct, Worrell the most stylish and Walcott a strong hitter of the ball. All were upset by the pace of Lindwall and Miller and Bill Johnston's variety and accuracy. Worrell, a most charming man, was to return as captain nine years later and take part in, perhaps, the most famous Test series of all.

The three Australian star pace bowlers carried all before them with 64 of the wickets that fell to the ball, Bill Johnston once again proving his value and justifying a remark made to me by the late 'Ginty' Lush that he was 'the best of the lot'. Valentine captured more wickets than anyone with 24 at 28.79, but Ramadhin fell away after a good start. His 14 wickets cost just below 50 apiece. But the series was far from being as onesided as Australia's winning margin of 4 games to 1 would indicate. The visitors lost two Tests narrowly—three wickets in Brisbane and one wicket in Melbourne. Gomez, in modern days, would have been difficult to go past as 'man of the series'—324 runs at 36, and 18 wickets at 14.22; although Miller certainly would have been in contention too—362 runs at 40 and 20 wickets at 20. There were only five three-figure scores in the five games, two of these to Lindsay Hassett.

A return visit from the South Africans was arranged for the 1952–53 season and this, with the interstate games, would form the basis for the 1953 visit to England for another Ashes series. The pre-war Australian stars who had adorned our post-war teams were now gradually fading from the scene. Hassett was well into his thirties, Morris and Lindwall would turn 31 in the coming summer and Keith Miller would be almost 33. Bill Johnston would be 30 and Ian Johnson 34. All these players still had lots of cricket left but neglect of up and coming players would be unwise. The most promising of these, and mature for his age with two overseas tours already under his belt, was Neil Harvey, just 25-years-old by 1953. Others from whom much was expected were Ken Archer, Richie Benaud and Graeme Hole. Langley, from South Australia, was preferred to Tallon in the final Test against the West Indies and seemed set to edge the Queenslander out in coming series. Don Tallon was 30-years-old before he gained a place in an Australian team although most people considered him the leading wicket-keeper in the land as far back as 1938 when both Barnett and Charlie Walker were taken to England instead of him. Walker died flying over Germany in 1942, and Ben Barnett, a charming man, was a prisoner of war in Japanese hands for three years. It would be churlish to begrudge these two their 1938 trip, but it would be hard to rate them as better wicket-keepers than Tallon at that time. Barnes and Moroney, for different reasons, were out of favour and their international careers were at an end.

Of the South Africans who played against Australia in 1949–50 at home, only Melle, John Waite, Cheetham, John Watkins and Tayfield survived. Nourse, the two Rowans and Mitchell had retired, McCarthy's action was suspect and the others had fallen by the wayside. The team, skippered by the well-liked Jack Cheetham, was at the outset given little chance of making a game of it in Australia, let alone of winning a Test match. In the upshot, the series was squared at two games all, with the fourth Test drawn. The visitors welded into a fielding side quite the equal of the Australians, and in Russell Endean, Roy McLean and Ken Funston had unearthed batsmen of top class. John Waite proved the equal of Langley behind the stumps and was more than useful with the bat. Tayfield was the best spinner on either side and had a memorable tour with 30 Test wickets. The difference between the two teams was Neil Harvey who resumed where he had left off three years before in South Africa. Once again he returned Bradman-like figures: 834 runs at 92.67.

Arthur Morris had a reasonable season in Tests and a very satisfactory one overall, although the magic three figures eluded him until the bitter end when he scored 105 for the 1953 Australians in Western Australia en route for England. In the Tests, he was fourth in the batting averages of those who played in all Tests. Harvey was out of sight and behind him, far behind, came McDonald and Hassett.

Arthur started the season well with 95 and 38 in successive matches against Queensland. In Sydney against the visiting South Africans, he fell twice to Tayfield for 55 and 39. In this game a seventeen year old, Ian Craig, made a notable entry on the international scene with an aggressive 71. The captain in this match was Keith Miller and the honour seesawed between him and Arthur during the season. This never affected the personal friendship of the two men. Arthur was preferred as vice-captain for Australian teams of the time.

Against Victoria Arthur scored 69, falling to his old foe Bill Johnston, but in Adelaide he failed twice, falling to an orthodox left-arm spinner, John Manning, for 10 and 15. Manning's talents were lost to Australian cricket when he took off for a career in English county cricket where he performed with distinction.

In the first Test at Brisbane, Arthur made 29 and 58 in a match of moderate scoring except for Neil Harvey's contribution of 109, his fifth century in six Tests against South Africa. Australia won by 96 runs after setting the tourists 337 to win. Funston and 'Jackie' McGlew offered stern resistance but Lindwall got up a full head of steam to take 5–60.

The Melbourne Test brought the Australians back to the field with a jerk. The visitors batted first but trailed by 16 on the first innings. Morris made a useful 43 for Australia, falling to a freakish caught and bowled effort by Tayfield, and Harvey didn't score a century.

Arthur's dismissal caused him some embarrassment. The Springbok captain, Cheetham, brought Endean into a silly mid-off position. Morris regarded this as insulting and belted Tayfield's next ball straight at the unfortunate fieldsman. It hit him hard on the shoulder and flew high behind the umpire at the bowler's end. Tayfield, turning quickly at the end of his follow through, raced back and hurled himself at the ball, catching it one handed, lying on his back. It was no consolation to

Arthur that Endean, leaving for repairs to his shoulder, accompanied him from the field.

Batting again, Russell Endean batted through the innings for 162 not out of a total of 388. Endean was a splendid opening batsman, an acrobatic fieldsman and a capable understudy to John Waite behind the stumps. Batting again, chasing 372, the Australians fell 82 short. Tayfield had the fine figures of 7–81 and was becoming something of a problem with his pinpoint accuracy supported by some dazzling fielding and catching. Morris's dismissal for 1 was disappointing. Michael Melle posted John Watkins at leg slip and Arthur tickled a good length ball pitched on the leg stump to Watkins for a straightforward catch.

In the return match for the State against the Springboks, Arthur was out to all-rounder Anton Murray, who bowled medium pacers of some variety and disposed of Morris, Carroll and de Courcey in quick time. Young Ian Craig then took charge and went on to make a thrilling and often spectacular double century before Keith Miller closed the innings at 7–416. Craig was the youngest Australian to score a double century in a first-class match and compiled his 213 in just over six hours with 22 fours.

The third and fourth Tests followed close on the heels of each other and there was no joy for Arthur until the second innings of the Adelaide match. Harvey blitzed the visitors at Sydney with 190. Arthur Morris had to be content with 18, bowled by John Watkins, who was proving himself a more than handy all-rounder with runs and wickets provided usually when they were badly needed. Australia scored 443 in this match and bowled the South Africans out for 173 and 232. This performance was easily the tourists' worst in the series. Funston made 56 in the first innings and Roy McLean 65 in the second. McLean was an exciting right-handed batsman, especially strong on the hook and the cut and always looking for runs. He was the greatest crowd pleaser of his time in South African cricket. Impetuosity frequently cost him his wicket before he was properly set, and his Test match batting average of 33.95 is an inadequate reflection of his natural ability.

Australia had the best of the Adelaide match. Batting first, Hassett, McDonald and Harvey (again) scored heavily in a total of 530. Morris was out for 1 caught by Endean off the lively Fuller. The South Africans fought gamely to avoid the follow on with 387, forcing Australia to bat again. The name of Benaud popped up as a bowler to be watched in this match. He had played in one game against the West Indies the preceding summer without setting the world on fire, but in this match took 4–118, giving support to the ever-reliable Bill Johnston who had 5–110. Australia batted briskly in their second innings to enable Hassett to close the innings and try to snatch victory. Arthur after four successive failures batted in something like his best style, aided by a stroke or two of luck, for a lively 77 before the ubiquitous Endean made it look easy as he pocketed an edge off Michael Melle's bowling. Harvey, not surprisingly, scored 116. The South Africans must have almost reached the point where they would have given him 100 runs as long as he undertook not to bat. Chasing 376, the South Africans were saved from defeat by the clock, the match ending in a draw with the visitors still 200 short of victory and with only 4 wickets standing.

The final Test in Melbourne was a match to be savoured. In winning it, the South Africans became only the third side in history to win a Test after facing a first innings total of over 500. Neil Harvey scored 205 in the first innings and passed Bradman's best-ever series total against South Africa. Morris, sacrificing his wicket, was run out for 99 in a mix-up with Ian Craig, a once only event in his career and an experience which still pains him. Ian Craig, at 17 years 8 months, the youngest player to represent Australia, had a memorable Test scoring 53 and 47.

Morris's innings earned widespread praise both for its quality and the unselfishness which terminated it. He was now batting in his best style with bowlers of all types finding it a problem to place run-saving fields for him.

Five South Africans passed 50 in their first innings. Roy McLean had a great match, with 81 and 76 not out, being there when his side knocked off the 297 runs wanted for victory with the loss of only 4 wickets. This was indeed a famous victory which levelled the series at two matches all. Although it would probably be agreed that Australia was the better side, with a moral win in the Sydney Test, the team of 'learners' from the Veldt had certainly learnt quickly and well, and demonstrated what great fielding and an equal sharing of runs and wickets between all participants, with virtually no 'star players', could accomplish. Arthur Morris made 44 in Australia's modest second innings of 209 and finished the series on a high note.

The batting averages, apart from Harvey on 92 and Craig on 50 (for only two innings), found Morris fifth with 370 runs at 41, a result much improved on his efforts against the West Indies. A G Moyes noted that Arthur's early 'dismal' form had led in some quarters to calls for his omission. But 'the turning point came in the second innings of the Adelaide Test when, with runs needed quickly, Morris reverted to his previous habits and attacked the bowling, playing his drives and finding the form he'd (temporarily) mislaid', Moyes contended. In the final Test, with 99 and 44, his faith in himself was restored which gave general pleasure to everybody.

Morris's batting still bore the unmistakable hallmark of class. If his performances fell short of the sensational overtures played in 1946–47 and 1948, this was and is still not unusual. Walter Hammond, in 1934, batted eight times for 162 but blossomed again in 1936 and 1938. Trumper and Macartney had similarly lean seasons. Morris's low point was the series against the West Indies and he was, hopefully, on the upgrade.

In Endean, McLean and McGlew, the Springboks had launched players of some class. Funston did not fulfil his early promise but McLean and McGlew adorned the scene for some time. The latter was never a player who would persuade anyone to lose his job to go and watch him bat, but his value to South African cricket was considerable. But the main glory of the side was its fielding. They equalled, and possibly surpassed, the Australians in this department and the catching frequently put paid abruptly to many threatening partnerships. Morris had experience of this. Cheetham, the captain, played an inspiring role in all this and was widely admired on and off the field. And so they went home with the best record of any country against Australia in the five Test series played since the war (six if you count the brief tour of New Zealand in 1946). This surprised everybody, not least the South Africans, and they would never again be regarded as 'easy beats' by anyone.

The Lion Triumphs
ENGLAND 1953

ashes homeward bound

THE COMING TOUR OF ENGLAND IN THE 1953 European summer was keenly awaited, it now being apparent that England were over their post-war fragility and that some stern encounters could be expected. And so it turned out. Freddie Brown's team of spare parts in Australia in 1950 had clawed its way to a victory in the final Test, something which had not been expected when the tour began. Compton's failures had influenced the series greatly and, had he shown his usual form, the margin in Australia's favour of 4 to 1 would almost certainly have been reduced.

In England, there was some satisfaction in the thought that the scourge of the four preceding tours, Don Bradman, would only be present as a reporter—as one would expect, he carried out these duties for the *Daily Mail* in the same thorough and thoughtful manner that he'd followed throughout his life. The other bonus, from England's point of view, was that Sid Barnes, 'the Artful Dodger' as Ray Robinson dubbed him, was 'persona non grata' with Australian officialdom and had, in characteristic fashion, advised them what they could do with the game and its various appurtenances. It scarcely mattered who replaced Bradman and Barnes, England could hardly be worse off. Indeed, after South Africa squared the series in 1952–53 in Australia, the betting might have been close to even money or even slightly odds on England.

The Australian selectors, Messrs Jack Ryder, Bill Brown and Phil Ridings, announced the team on February 12, shortly before the South Africans headed home. Those chosen were:

HASSETT A L	VIC	(CAPTAIN)
MORRIS A R	NSW	(VICE-CAPTAIN)
ARCHER R G	QLD	
BENAUD R	NSW	
CRAIG I D	NSW	
DAVIDSON A L	NSW	
DE COURCY J H	NSW	
HARVEY R N	VIC	
HILL J C	VIC	
HOLE G B	SA	
JOHNSTON W A	VIC	
LANGLEY G R A	SA	
LINDWALL R R	NSW	
McDONALD C C	VIC	
MILLER K R	NSW	
RING D T	VIC	
TALLON D	QLD	

Archer, Benaud, Craig and Davidson were comparative newcomers while de Courcy had not played in a Test. But the big surprise was the inclusion of J C Hill of whom few Englishmen had ever heard. He was a right-hand sharp purveyor of what appeared to be leg-breaks but which turned minimally. Most dangerous was his top spinner which bit and lifted. It was thought he might perform creditably on English wickets. Ian Johnson's omission surprised—he'd frequently proved troublesome to Len Hutton, a quality which some might think merited his inclusion no matter what. The side generally was viewed in England as a goodish distance below the 1948 outfit in overall quality, with the cautious proviso that it was never wise to underrate Australian teams who had often demonstrated an ability to 'match the hour' when it struck.

Tallon had made a meritorious comeback after illness but his ability was well short of the dazzling 1948 displays which led his contemporaries, to a man, and even so perceptive a critic as Bill O'Reilly, to rate him our best 'keeper ever.

Barnes's absence was especially pleasing to Alec Bedser who rated him the hardest batsman to dismiss. Barnes was also in England to write for the *Daily Express* and his comments were awaited with interest, remembering his battles with the Board of Control. Arthur Morris's lack of great success in the Tests since 1948 had left a slight question mark over him in English eyes, and his success or failure would certainly be critical to the team. The only other 'genuine' opener in the side was Colin McDonald. He'd performed very well against South Africa but some basic faults in his game were evident and the testing he would go through in England might expose them further. Hassett, ever reliable and versatile, was to be the 'spare opener'. As captain, Hassett was assured of a warm welcome and his soundness as a batsman probably made him the most important component in this side's batting line-up. If Morris should fail and Hassett (now approaching 40) be disabled, it wasn't hard to foresee difficulties. Much was expected of Harvey following his brilliant exhibitions since his last visit to England.

Australian critics (Oldfield and O'Reilly) thought the side the best available and, for England's part, the consensus was that they would be hard to beat but that England should carry the day.

As already mentioned, Arthur Morris scored his solitary century in the Australian season just ended on the way to England in Perth, with a fine 105 against Western Australia. He'd scored a few against Tasmania too, so that his season's output of 913 at 46 was not far from his best. The coming tour of England would have a special 'bonus' element for the tourists—Queen Elizabeth II was to be crowned and consequently the RMS *Orcades* was heavily laden with tourists as well as cricketers.

The tourists were welcomed by a distinguished band of officials and ex-cricketers, the most interesting being Douglas Jardine, not a favourite in his playing days but greatly mellowed by time and experience.

A P Herbert produced a lively piece of doggerel with which to greet the Australians at a Savoy function, the opening verse of which is worth quoting (with acknowledgments to Sir Alan):

> *Baby Bradman in her pouches*
> *Here's our favourite foe once more,*
> *And the wounded lion crouches*
> *With a most respectful roar.**

Morris scored 103 in the light-hearted match against a fairly strong invitation eleven at East Molesey. Arthur's century came in 80 minutes and recalled to spectators and press alike his dazzling form of 1948. This was a good start, marred by an accident to Bill Johnston who had to leave the field with a knee injury that proved quite serious and of some duration. The result was that the knee damage caused Bill to alter his delivery stride when bowling. It did not reduce his effectiveness greatly, but on the other hand it didn't improve it and he had to make adjustments.

Worcester had been initial hosts to Australia since 1930 when Bradman scored 236, with further double centuries in 1934 and 1938. In 1948, making some concession to the passage of time, Don was happy with a single century. From whatever angle the man's deeds are viewed, he was so much better than anyone else, before or since, that comparisons break down immediately. The weather was cold, the wicket slow after rain during the preceding week. After the County batted first, declaring at 7–333, the Australians made a bad start, losing 3–28, before Miller and Hole pulled the batting together with a double century partnership. Arthur Morris, who'd looked in complete control in reaching 18 was out trying to force Whitehead, a medium-pace exponent of the inswinger and cutter, to leg. The ball dipped away late and found a thick edge to fly straight to gully. Miller shepherded Hole through some early difficulties and later Ron Archer hit lustily to register a century on his first outing in England. Miller batted throughout and was 220 when Hassett closed the innings at 7–542. The match was drawn.

Morris didn't play at Leicester where Harvey, after a shaky start,

---

* The 'baby Bradman' mentioned is Ian Craig who was being hailed as another Bradman.

set the ground alight, first with Miller, then with Davidson. Leicester's two expatriate bowlers, Jack Walsh and Vic Jackson, both had unflattering figures. The Australians won by an innings, both Hill and Ring turning in good match results.

At Bradford, the 1948 Australians had gone as close to defeat as they would on that tour but on this occasion they defeated a depleted Yorkshire side, again by an innings. Sent in, the tourists reached 453 before Morris, who was captain for the match, closed the innings. Arthur, who'd taken Hole with him to open, got some useful practice with 57. He and Neil Harvey added 77 in quick time for the second wicket.

Miller was again not out for 159 and had the bizarre average of 421 to this point. Lindwall skittled Hutton in his first over, the 'Maestro' seeming to have some trouble separating his bat from a new pair of pads. This disaster affected the crowd deeply, and the silence of mingled disbelief and despair engulfed the ground as Len departed. He made amends in the second innings with a solid 65, during which he studied Hill's bowling closely. Benaud and Hill both did well in this match, Benaud staking an early claim for a Test spot with 7–46 from 19 overs in the first innings. Norman Yardley, former England captain and an on-driver of distinction, was not out in both innings for 50 and 56, but his efforts were insufficient to salvage his side from a fairly comprehensive defeat.

Interest in the Surrey match centred on the first encounter between the old sparring partners, Morris and Bedser. Batting first on a greenish wicket at the Oval, the home side was out for 58, Archer doing the damage with 6–26. Morris was captain in this match and the wicket having some moisture in it, and with Lindwall, Archer and Davidson at his disposal, thought it might prove profitable to pack the slip cordons on both sides of the wicket. Doing away with deep third man and deep fine leg, he placed four in orthodox slip positions and three as leg slips. Having brilliant catchers available in Benaud, Craig, Harvey, Hole and (when not bowling) Davidson and Archer and, correctly anticipating that the Surrey players would prop forward in their time honoured way, he simply required his bowlers to maintain a good length and the snicks would come. There was born, or reborn, 'the umbrella field' as dubbed by the English press. Keith Miller recalls that Keith Carmody had first used it when playing for the Services team in 1945 but both he and Arthur are quick to acknowledge that such fields limit and stultify stroke play, boring spectators and frustrating batsmen. Both welcomed the decree, later passed, limiting to two the number of fieldsmen behind square leg. Morris was playing well until Bedser, varying his stock out-swinger (to the left-hander) with a leg-cutter, found an inside edge as Morris moved across the wicket and bowled him behind his legs for 20. Bedser added Harvey, Craig and Benaud to finish with 4–60 out of Australia's 256. This was good news for England supporters, despite an innings win to Australia.

At Fenners, which is a pleasant ground adjacent to Cambridge University which, in its turn, borders the dawdling Cam River, the Australians continued on their winning way. The strip of this idyllic ground is usually one which bowlers regard with unadulterated distaste, so courteous is it to the batsmen. So it was a good effort by the students to see the Australians off before six on the first day. Morris skippered the side and, batting on a couch 'stuffed with runs' as Cardus would say, they were all out at 5.40 for 383. All the batsmen played in a relaxed manner against an ordinary attack apart from Robin Marlar, an off spinner of some note who finished with 5–139 from 36 overs. Morris occupied one end with more care than some of the others, particularly Miller, who opened with his acting captain and seemed in some haste to depart the scene for nearby Newmarket where there was a race meeting. Arthur batted for two and a half hours for a thoughtful 79 which, if not in his best vein, certainly provided him with necessary practice. He finally dragged a Marlar full toss on to his stumps. Archer and Ring ripped the University's batting apart, Ring with 9 wickets for the match, Archer 7. Lindwall was used sparingly and Miller bowled only five overs in the match, which was comfortably won midway through the third day by an innings and 106 runs. Raman Subba Row, an England player a few years hence, batted impressively in the second innings for 41.

Returning to London for the MCC match at Lord's, the Australians were met by a strong side which sported eleven probable, certain or possible Test candidates. Lindwall slipped himself, really for the first time on tour, in a short but devastating opening spell in which he removed Reg Simpson, David Sheppard and Denis Compton. With Hassett still on the sidelines and the opening day washed out by rain, Morris sent MCC in on a grey, cold Monday morning and saw his tactics vindicated by some fine bowling, good catching and, it must be said, poor batting from players of whom more resistance could reasonably be expected. Only three players got to double figures and the side could only reach a dismal 89. But the Australians did little better. Morris was brilliantly caught at forward short leg by David Sheppard from an authentic stroke when he was 6. The new boys, Davidson and Benaud, with Lindwall, restored some dignity to the batting which petered out at an unimpressive 179. Miller fired in the MCC second innings with 4–47, but there was encouraging batting from Compton and a stern not out effort by Trevor Bailey, never known to surrender his wicket at any time. The game ended in a draw, the Australians 2–13 in their second innings and Morris not out 4.

Christ Church ground at Oxford competes in charm and beauty with Fenners at Cambridge. The Australians defeated the Oxonians by an innings and 86 runs. Morris failed again and, with McDonald out for 0, the Australian openers had yet to register a significant opening partnership on tour. Morris made 15, and at one stage the tourists were 4–62. De Courcy made a fine maiden century and Hole and Ron Archer kept him company while a respectable 330 was reached. The students offered little resistance in either innings and all the bowlers got their share of wickets.

Arthur Morris's form was giving one and all cause for concern at this stage. He had batted seven times with one 'not out' for 198 runs, at an average of 33. At the corresponding time of the 1948 tour he'd scored 603 runs at 86. And the end of this 'bad trot' was still some distance away.

With Hassett fit, Morris missed the Minor Counties game in which Neil Harvey made 109 on a pitch which was damp at first and then dusty. Fingleton wrote that it was the finest innings he'd yet seen Harvey play. Ben Barnett skippered the Counties side—he'd settled in Buckinghamshire after the war and was still keeping wickets.

Old Trafford had lived up to its reputation during the preceding 'Roses' match against Yorkshire with storm and tempest followed by torrential rain which washed out the first day of the Australian's match against Lancashire. In the remaining two days, Morris made 29 out of his side's 298. He was out, hooking, to a marvellous boundary catch after Statham had given him a few anxious moments. Arthur always considered Statham a fine bowler and, indeed in this match, the Australians considered him the best pace bowler they'd met in England and it seemed likely he'd be pushing Trueman for a Test place. Harvey scored another century but not in his best style until the latter part of his innings. Lindwall was called for 'dragging' by Umpire Corrall. Bill O'Reilly was critical of this decision, the first time Lindwall had been cited during the tour. He bowled pretty well for 4–41 and was clearly working up to top speed. The match was drawn.

Morris failed again against Notts, caught behind off the medium pace of Jepson—the report of the game stated that he was playing across the line. Bruce Dooland, former South Australian and Australian leg spinner, bowled economically for the County, taking 1–83 from 34 overs. This game was limited to two days to enable the tourists to return to London for the coronation of Elizabeth II. The result was a draw.

Morris missed the Sussex match at Hove, where Maurice Tate spent a good slice of his life coming upwind and confusing batsmen from all parts of the globe for so long. Of his 2784 first-class wickets, it would be no exaggeration to imagine that possibly 1000 of them were taken at Hove or Brighton. Harvey, Hassett and McDonald all scored centuries in a drawn game.

The picturesque Southampton ground was the scene of a welcome return to form for Arthur Morris. Captaining the side again, he scored 55 and 50. In the first innings, Arthur and Neil Harvey hammered the Hampshire bowlers to add 124 in under even time. Harvey made another century. In the second innings, Arthur made 50 in under an hour, hitting three sixes and six fours. The Australians won comfortably despite some fine hitting in the second innings by former West Indian player Roy Marshall who bettered Morris's effort, smiting five sixes and five fours in a memorable 71.

Trent Bridge, Nottingham, is a ground which has seen some famous events. Home patch of Larwood and Voce, scene of Charlie Macartney's 345 against the County in 1921, all made in one day and, perhaps most cherished of all for Australians, the place where Stan McCabe scored 232 in 235 minutes in a Test Match in 1938. Bradman considered this still, in 1990, the greatest innings he ever saw. The 1953 Australians came to Nottingham for the first Test with a run of successes quite comparable with those enjoyed by Bradman's 1948 team. England's selectors were restricted by the lack of form of their number one fast bowler, Fred Trueman, whose opportunities had been limited because of his duties in the Royal Air Force. Tony Lock had an injured spinning finger and some of the established players like Peter May and Tom Graveney had done little to this point in the season. Bill Edrich had an injury, and the opening support for Hutton fell on Don Kenyon of Worcestershire, the sole century maker against the Australians to date. Many would have preferred Washbrook. The eleven chosen were: Hutton, Kenyon, Simpson, Compton, Graveney, May, Bailey, Evans, Wardle, Bedser and Tattersall. The last named was preferred to Laker but few would consider that he was the better bowler.

The Australians included Benaud, Davidson and Hill and the others virtually chose themselves except for the omission of McDonald, which left Morris's opening partner a matter for conjecture. In the event, Graeme Hole was thrown in at the deep end only to be bowled twice by Bedser for 0 and 5. Hole's high back lift would always make his choice as an opener something of a gamble.

Hassett won the toss on a dull day but on a pitch which looked likely to yield runs. Morris and Hassett and Miller staved off total humiliation on this day. Morris proceeded safely to 67 against a rampant Bedser who was moving the ball late in the air and spitefully off the pitch in the heavy conditions. After a break for rain, Bedser caught Morris in front, 'on the shuffle' again said the scribes. It was an innings of value and gave Arthur much satisfaction following some fairly joyless experiences thus far. After Harvey went for 0, Miller and Hassett took the score to 237. Bedser, with the new ball, then took control and the next six wickets fell for 12 runs, Bedser finishing with 7–55. There were six zeros in the Australian total of 249. England came to the wicket in poor light and with Lindwall and Johnston in threatening mood. Miller was not fit to bowl. Lindwall removed Kenyon and Simpson quickly and England's hopes rested squarely with their two champions, Hutton and Compton. The latter unaccountably reached for a wide half-volley and steered it low to Morris at gully where he took a match-winning catch low to his right. Hutton carried on, clothed in despair, to 43 when he lifted his late cover drive fractionally to be caught. Johnny Wardle hit lustily but the others folded and the side was out for 144. Batting again the Australians put on a dismal display. Only Morris stood between his side and disaster. He played easily his finest innings of the tour, in grey conditions on a pitch which behaved variably and against an Alec Bedser with his tail truly up. Morris hit Bailey out of the attack and took the bat out on Wardle's slow left-hand spinners. At 60, Arthur was bowled around his legs by Tattersall—his runs had come up in 108 minutes while his partners contributed 21, the total being a sad-looking 6–81. To Arthur, this innings of 60 ranks equally with his match-winning 182 in the 1948 Leeds Test, as the two best Test match innings he played. Nobody else appeared to have too many clues as to what was going on and Bedser and Tattersall wrapped up the innings for 123, Bedser taking 7–44 and 14–99 in the match. England needed 229 runs to win and might well have scored them had not rain shortened the final day to two hours. Hutton batted with the ease that made many of us who saw him play wonder that he ever got out and was 60 not out when the match ended. The match was drawn but, given a full final day's play and Hutton's complete control, England could, with some justification, claim a moral victory.

At Chesterfield, rain curtailed a low scoring match, in which batsmen generally fared badly. Morris returned to the doldrums with 13 and 6. Occasional Test bowler, Cliff Gladwin, took 9 wickets in the match and Ring and Benaud were the main contributors for Australia, the latter with both bat and ball. With 197 and 146, it was an unconvincing batting display by the Australians on a seamer's wicket. The game was drawn.

Both Morris and Hassett missed the return match against Yorkshire at legendary Bramall Lane, Sheffield, and the Australians were led by Miller. Batting second, the Australians were saved from the follow on by a fluky innings of 86 from Miller who was dropped no fewer than six times. Hutton had a fine double with 67 and 84, batting 'with untroubled ease'. Of concern to the tourists was the decline of Don Tallon, who neither looked nor 'kept well. The match was drawn but might have earned Yorkshire a points win.

The Australians replaced Tallon with Langley for the Lord's Test and Ring came in for Hill, for a reason not readily discernible. Hill had acquitted himself well on tour and, even when not getting wickets, was a difficult man to get on top of with his speed through the air and low trajectory. For England, Statham came in for Tattersall, Willie Watson for May and Freddie Brown for Simpson. Brown, chairman of selectors, and in his 43rd year, was a controversial inclusion, but his playing under a professional captain hinted at a more democratic attitude in the hierarchy of the MCC.

The game, though drawn, was a tense and gritty struggle with England saved from defeat by the newcomer Watson and Trevor Bailey, after losing 4–73 chasing 343 to win.

Arthur Morris had another good Test with 30 and 89, falling once to Bedser and once to Compton. The weather was fine throughout and Hassett and Morris gave Australia a good start until Morris, playing soundly, was brilliantly stumped by Evans in a movement too quick for the eye to follow. That Evans habitually stood up to the wicket for Bedser, a fastish medium-paced bowler, is testimony to Evans's class and was, throughout the pair's playing careers, a great plus for Alec Bedser. This Morris dismissal was of considerable significance in the overall context of the match. Hassett went on to make 104, despite being interrupted by a leg injury, and both Harvey and Miller built firmly on the good start. Alan Davidson, batting at No 7, hit with power and judgment to give Australia a reasonable 346 despite the failure of the tail. Bedser finished with 5–105, one of his victims, Harvey, exhibiting some doubt at the leg before decision which saw him depart for 59.

After Lindwall got rid of Kenyon cheaply again, Hutton and Graveney played fluently to see England 1–177 at close of play. Lindwall bowled Graveney with the fourth ball of his warm-up over next morning. Graveney appeared still not to be quite awake and dragged a yorker on to his stumps. Compton joined Hutton and some fine cricket followed, with Lindwall and Miller throwing everything at two exceedingly accomplished batsmen. During this innings of 145, Hutton joined Hobbs, Sutcliffe and Hammond in scoring 2000 Test runs against Australia. Apart from Compton's 57, the rest of England's score card looked fairly dismal and the side was out for 372, Lindwall taking 5–66.

Australia's second innings started badly, Hassett being victim of a doubtful decision on a catch by Evans down the leg side. Hasset refrained from the histrionics attaching to these events nowadays. Keith Miller and Arthur Morris batted calmly and with purpose to bring the score to 1–96 at stumps. Morris relished the bowling of Freddie Brown, brought on by Hutton on the Monday morning to try to contain the batsmen and save his pace bowlers for the new ball. Morris played aggressively and, at 82, was dropped by Hutton at slip from the bowling of Wardle. But Arthur was not destined to be around when the new ball appeared. Hutton gave Compton a couple of overs and Arthur swung a long-hop high in the direction of square leg where Statham completed a miraculous running catch looking into the sun. Miller carried on to his century, first with Harvey then with Hole, until he pulled a Wardle delivery onto his wicket. Lindwall took the bowling by the neck, with 14 from a Wardle over and later, 13 from Bedser, an almost 'sacrilegious' punishment, one scribe said. Lindwall's 50 in 43 minutes brought Australia to 368, a lead of 342. The rest of the day belonged to Australia, with Lindwall again in the van. Kenyon and Hutton fell to the great bowler, the latter reaching for and snicking a half volley to slip where Hole pocketed it. Graveney then failed to remove his bat from a Johnston delivery which he misread and was caught by Langley at full stretch. At this stage England were 3–12 and there were heavy hearts at cricket headquarters.

Compton and Watson played out time until stumps with England 3–20. The final day saw Australia frustrated and England uplifted by two defiant innings in extremely trying circumstances. After Compton left at 73, any hope of victory was dashed and it remained for Bailey and Watson to survive. Watson, an agreeable and phlegmatic Yorkshireman exhibited the tenacity and singlemindedness for which his home county is famous, and Bailey was a thorn in the side of Australia as he would often be again. Watson survived until almost 6pm, Bailey until shortly after and Brown and Wardle sealed the result. It had been a splendid match, albeit drawn. Morris's good Test form continued and he was now batting in something close to his 1948 style. Bedser had another eight-wicket bag to give him 22 for the two Tests completed, and Brown had a creditable double with 22 and 28 and 4–82 in Australia's second innings.

At Bristol, home of the Gloucestershire County Club and scene of many triumphs of the late great Walter Hammond, the Australians broke their run of drawn games by beating the County by 9 wickets. Tom Graveney got a few runs in the first innings and George Emmett scored 141 in the second. Emmett had won fame (or notoriety) as the selectors' choice to replace Len Hutton for the Old Trafford Test of 1948—surely one of the most outrageous selection blunders in history. Arthur Morris did not maintain his Test match form but looked good while he was there. At 26 he pulled the off spinner Cook, straight to Emmett at midwicket. De Courcy and Harvey stabilised the innings after six wickets fell for 136. Harvey hit 22 fours in a display dazzling even by his standards, and finished with 141. De Courcy was unlucky to be out at 97. Australia were all out for 402.

The County's second innings of 297 left Australia 33 runs to get, which they succeeded in doing with the loss of Richie Benaud. Morris and Tallon were not out.

Leading the side against Northampton Arthur scored 80. In this game he made the acquaintance of Frank Tyson who turned out to be quite the fastest English bowler the Australians had faced since the war. With a high action off a run which seemed to start from the sightboard, he was a frightening sight indeed, seeming to be close enough to shake hands with the striker at the end of his follow-through. Tyson remembers this occasion with relish. He recalls Freddie Brown placing an aggressive field with himself at short leg. 'I thundered in from the end of my marathon approach', said Frank, 'and after my first over, I'd captured the wickets of McDonald and Hole and hit Morris a couple of wringing blows on the thigh with short pitched balls. Each time I struck Morris, Freddie chuckled and from his short leg position, asked Artie how he liked being on the receiving end.'

When de Courcy fell to Nobby Clark who bowled fast lefthand, Australia were 3–10, and with Miller and Hassett resting, all depended on Morris and Harvey. The latter, like McCabe, only knew one way to deal with this sort of crisis—he attacked, quickly seeing Tyson off, and with Morris playing second fiddle, the two added 100 in eight-five minutes, of which Harvey made 71. The pair were not separated until the position had been stabilised at 185, Harvey scoring 118 in two hours. Arthur Morris's part in this partnership was very important and he looked sure to register his first century of the tour when, at 80, he fell to another expatriate, George Tribe, a left hand off spinner in the line of Fleetwood–Smith, but rather more accurate.

Australia's innings ended at 323 and the County crumbled quickly for 141 and 120. Archer took 7–56 in the first innings, Ring 5–46 in the second and the tourists won by an innings and 62 runs.

For the Old Trafford Test England for various reasons omitted Kenyon, Brown, Statham (injured) and Tattersall. Bill Edrich came back for Kenyon, Simpson for Brown, Laker for Tattersall and Trueman for Statham. The Lancashire folk were not over impressed at the continued overlooking of their own Cyril Washbrook, but Bill Edrich, a tried and true fighter, was a good selection as opening partner for Hutton.

Bill Johnston had knee trouble and was replaced by Archer. De Courcy came in for Benaud and Hill for Ring. With rain about, England omitted Trueman and went into the match without a genuine pace bowler. On the other hand, Australia played Lindwall, Archer and Davidson.

As usual, rain interfered with the result so the game ended on a note that was almost farcical and unworthy of a Test match. Hassett won the toss for the third time and opened with Morris on a blustery, cheerless Manchester day. In his second over, Bedser bowled what Cardus would call a 'sinful' outswinger to Morris, which cut back and fizzed.

Morris did well to get a bat on to it at all but not well enough to stop it rolling on to his stumps. He was generally considered to have been unlucky. Morris, on the other hand, regards this as his most embarrassing dismissal; the backspin on the ball as he hit it into the pitch caused it to bounce a couple of times and hit the stumps while he watched on helplessly. With Australia 3–48, the situation cried out for drastic remedies. Who better then to enter the fray than Neil Harvey? He had some luck this day. He played and missed a few times but never deviated from his intention to push the score along. With Hole playing confidently, the pair added 173 for the fourth wicket. Harvey was out for 122 in 4½ hours, his second century against England but his eleventh overall, the other nine mainly at the expense of the South Africans. The Australians reached 318 with little help from the tail after de Courcy made 41. Bedser had another five-wicket haul and bowled quite beautifully.

Apart from Hutton and Compton, there was little joy for England supporters when they batted. Hassett, realising that Bill Edrich had never faced Hill, brought him into the attack after Lindwall had bowled a mere three overs. Edrich groped forward to Hill's third ball and edged it straight to Hole at slip. Compton was at his best and, with Hutton, added 94 runs when Compton was caught at the wicket just before the close for as good a 45 as he ever made. Hutton fell leg before to Lindwall and England went in at a shaky 4–126.

Rain prevented any play on the Monday and there was much talk of dropping Manchester from the Test match agenda, or at least varying the time at which it was played. In this match, the time lost virtually ruled out any purpose in the cricket that followed on the Tuesday (again rain interrupted). The England innings meandered on to its close, enlivened only by a boisterous knock from Godfrey Evans. At 5pm the innings finished at 276, leaving Australia an hour to bat. The tourists lost 8–35 in this hour, nobody reached double figures and the atmosphere had a decidedly picnic air. The wickets taken in this innings should scarcely be counted in assessing averages, even less when comparing bowlers. Wardle had the extraordinary figures of 5–2–7–4, Laker 9–5–11–2 and Bedser 4–1–14–2. It really didn't make much sense.

The Australians flew to the Hague for a one-day match against a Dutch side. Everybody enjoyed the visit, with hospitality lavish and almost fanatical enthusiasm for cricket in the vicinity of the Hague. Arthur made a lively 70 out of the Australians' 279 and eight Australians, including Tallon, had a bowl in the Dutch Eleven's score of 122.

Arthur had a rest from the Middlesex match at Lord's. Bill Edrich got a few in the County's first innings and nearly all the Australians got useful practice in the 416 scored. Poor Ian Craig, still in the horrors, was out for 2. Lindwall took his fiftieth tour wicket, and Hassett was criticised for not closing his side's innings earlier when he had a sizeable lead. Hassett's argument was that he was not keen to give Compton and Edrich, particularly, batting practice against his bowlers in a match short-ened by rain anyway. On the other hand, it can be argued that, as the cliché so aptly puts it, 'the game's the thing'.

The Headingley ground at Leeds held happy memories for Arthur Morris, for it was here, five years before, that he and Don Bradman had won a match in sensational fashion on a wearing wicket on the final day, when Australia lost only 3 wickets in chasing over 400. Arthur had scored 182 on that famous day. In a low-scoring game this time, he was destined not to repeat that effort.

For England Tony Lock, fit at last, came in for Wardle. Lock was a splendid left-hand bowler, far more aggressive in method and demean-our than the amiable Johnny Wardle. Although Statham was included in the twelve instead of Trueman, like Trueman, he was made twelfth man. There were no changes in the Australian twelve that played at Old Trafford, but Hill was made twelfth man and Benaud returned. The Australians did well in this match and won at least a moral victory. England were dismissed late on the last day after a long rearguard fight which left Australia 177 runs to win in two hours. To everyone's sur-prise, they accepted the challenge and with Morris, Harvey and Hole batting brilliantly, reached 4–147 when time ran out. Morris was in full cry when he missed a driveable ball from Laker and was stumped with great panache and ease by Evans for 38.

In this match, Hutton failed twice—bowled third ball for 0 in the first innings and caught at the wicket by Langley off Archer for 25 in the second. Edrich, Graveney and Compton all scored useful runs in one or other innings and Lindwall had 8 wickets for the match. Harvey and Hole had good doubles for Australia and Morris fell for 10 to Bedser in the first innings, caught at leg slip by Tony Lock, a specialist in that position. Bedser finished with another good bag of wickets—7 for the match. This gave him 36 in four games, a phenomenal performance. Maurice Tate's 38 in Australia in 1924 was surely under threat, with a match to go. For a drawn game, this Leeds match had plenty of excitement, even if the overall standard was a little lower than the 1948 series.

Hurrying back to London for the return match against Surrey at The Oval, the Australians were a little weary from the sleepless train trip following hard on a grinding Test match. Hassett lost the toss but the lads were cheered up by Bill Johnston's return to active duty after a fairly long lay-off. Rain again intervened on the first day. Peter May made a splendid 56 and Ray Lindwall and Johnston had good spells with the ball, the latter taking 4–51 from 27 overs. Arthur Morris batted beautifully in similar fashion to his second innings at Leeds. He carved up all the bowlers and was out driving Surridge, caught at mid-off for 67. Arthur recalls that in this innings he deliberately set out to hit the younger Stuart Surridge for an over of sixes. He pulled the first delivery, on-drove the second, both for six but Surridge had the last word, pitching his third delivery wide of the off stump. Arthur drove but mishit slightly to be caught. Harvey made 100 in two hours and Ian Craig, when batting well, was run out for 16. Harvey's century was his ninth of the tour and Bradman's tally of 13 on the 1938 tour looked like getting a shake. The game was drawn.

The weather at Swansea for the Glamorgan match was warm and sunny and Neil Narvey honoured the occasion and the famous ground with a dazzling 180 in 167 minutes. Davies, the wicket-keeper, said that it was the finest innings by a left-hander he'd ever seen. Glamorgan batted first and were out for 201, a resurgent and lively Bill Johnston taking 6–63. When Australia batted Morris, acting captain, unleashed a barrage of shots to all points going to 48 in 45 minutes before he was leg before to off-spinner, Jim McConnon. The account of this match remarks that 'Morris's batting at this stage of the tour had to be seen to be believed; no one could bowl a length to him'. If the centuries failed to come, the 40s, 50s and 70s he was churning out in some profusion were giving much pleasure to all those lucky enough to see him bat.

McConnon, a very tidy bowler, had the fine figures of 7–165 from 35 overs in what could fairly be described as a batting landslide, at least while Morris and Harvey were batting. A notable event, too, in the Australian innings, was a half century by Ian Craig—it wasn't flawless but it gave general approval, for the young man had borne his endless run of misfortune with dignity and a wry sense of humour. The Glamorgan second innings, with the help of some rain, hung on long enough to draw the match. Wilf Wooller, the Glamorgan skipper of some fame, was 71 not out.

Morris had a spell against Warwickshire. Hassett was criticised for not taking up the home skipper's challenging second innings closure at 3–76 which left Australia 166 to win in 170 minutes on a wicket taking spin and Eric Hollies in the Warwick attack. Hassett declined the challenge, considering the task impossible and not wishing his side to suffer defeat with the fifth and deciding Test a short way off. As it was, the Australians were 5–53 at the close, Hassett watching his colleagues fold was there at the finish.

The return match at Old Trafford against the Red Rose folk was played in beautiful late summer weather and was won comfortably by the Australians by seven wickets. Arthur, still in scintillating form, made a lightning 64 before going leg before to Tattersall. Neil Harvey failed, which was almost more newsworthy than if he'd scored a century. At the beginning of his innings of 64, Arthur took 20 from Statham's opening over including a six over square leg. Statham was omitted from the England side for the final Test and told Arthur, without rancour that he considered that his cavalier treatment was influential in his (Statham's) omission. Davidson and Ring hit merrily to lift the total to a highly entertaining 372 in which Tattersall took 5–80.

Lindwall and Co dispatched the home side speedily for 184, although Tallon's continued indifferent form seemed to carry over to the Australians' fielding which was unusually untidy. Following on, the County did better, Jack Ikin and expatriate Australian, Ken Grieves, batting very well, the latter very strong off the back foot in the Australian fashion. The total of 292 left Australia with 105 to win, which they managed with the loss of three wickets. Morris was in a hurry again and hurled the bat at anything within reach for another eye-catching 38. Tattersall took all three wickets that fell to give him 8–106 in the match. Tattersall, an above average specimen of the off spinning club which had members in every county, was never quite as good as Laker, in whose shadow he was destined to operate at international level.

At Southend the Australians crushed Essex in two days. Although they did not equal the 1948 side's 721 in a day, they set about the attack with relish on a first-day pitch which played perfectly. After Morris tore Bailey and Preston into shreds to race to 33 in less than even time, and Harvey failed again, Hole and de Courcy added 155 for the third wicket. This set the tone for the hard hitters of the middle order and de Courcy went on to make a highly entertaining 164 in just under 3½ hours. The innings closed at 477.

Next day, as Bill O'Reilly noted, the wicket turned traitor when the County batted. It crumbled badly and the spinners, with Bill Johnston confirming his fitness with a mixture of fast and slow left-arm seamers and spinners, bowled Essex out for 129 and 136 to give Australia a crushing victory.

Kennington Oval, the ground graced for so long by that greatest of English batsmen, J B Hobbs, has long been the venue for the final Test in the Ashes series, and this year it was to be an especially significant and important occasion. Honours in the series to date, with no decision in any of the four games played, were fairly even. The standard of cricket played had been variable, on the whole rather below that of 1948. Arthur Morris had had little Test match success since the Lord's Test in June and his performances bore little resemblance to those of 1948 when he carried all before him. In the match now to be played, the pattern was the same as it had been in his previous four innings. However it would surely linger long in his memory, if only because he happened to be thrown the ball to bowl the last over of the match to give England its first home victory since the annihilation of 1938. On that occasion, Hutton scored 364 and England won by an innings and 579 runs—a margin which does not bear thinking about. In the year of the coronation of Queen Elizabeth II it was, perhaps, appropriate for the Ashes to return home.

For the Australians, Ron Archer came in for Benaud. England picked an extra bowler in Trueman at the expense of Watson and replaced Simpson with Peter May. This was probably the best balanced side of the series with five specialist batsmen, four specialist bowlers, and a redoubtable all-rounder in Trevor Bailey, plus Godfrey Evans whose wicket-keeping had been exemplary. The absence of a genuine spinner (other than Jack-of-all-trades, Bill Johnston) in the Australian side was perhaps significant as Laker and Lock scythed through the Australian second innings with 9 wickets between them. Bedser, for the only time in the series, had to take second place with 0–24.

Morris opened with Hassett who'd won his fifth successive toss. Morris was technically dropped at leg-slip by Compton off Trueman's bowling before he'd scored and there was a collective exhalation of air, half breath, half sigh, from the watching thousands. Arthur was lacking in confidence despite his recent good form and both batsmen were playing a fraction late at Trueman's extra pace. But it was Bedser who straightened one to find Morris's leg in direct line with the off stump and he left after an unconvincing, out of character, 16. Hassett proceeded calmly with moderate assistance from Harvey. Hole, Lindwall and Davidson scored valuable runs late in the innings which closed at 275.

England progressed well after a shaky start in the late afternoon light. On the Monday morning Lindwall and Miller unleashed a ferocious assault resulting in Edrich's departure leg before at 37. Both May and Hutton played and missed more frequently than they'd have liked but carried the total on to 137. Compton and Graveney both failed but the ubiquitous Bailey stiffened the lower order so that England reached 306 after some bad moments early in the innings. Lindwall had 4–70 and the tirelessly persevering and accurate Johnston bowled 45 overs to finish with 3–94. Among post-war bowlers there have been few as good as, let alone better than, Bill Johnston.

England, per the medium of Messrs Lock and Laker, the Surrey twins, were now about to administer the coup de grace. The Australian second innings was something of a procession once these two virtuosi were brought into the attack. Arthur saw Hassett, Harvey, Hole and Miller all depart in varying degrees of confusion on a wicket taking a little spin, but slow spin. Then it was his turn after a soundly compiled 26—playing back and across to Lock he was leg before to that gentleman's exuberant delight and the delirium of the crowd—Australia 5–61. Archer hit defiantly for a game 49 and, with Davidson, a batsman of similar outlook, knocked the spinners out of the attack for a time. At tea, Australia were 6–131 and there were some mild palpitations in English hearts. But soon after the adjournment, Lock bowled Davidson with a scorcher which bit and turned quite sharply. Archer soon followed, caught at slip, and the end was quick. Australia, all out 162, left England 132 to win, Laker having taken 4–75 and Lock 5–45. There were widespread doubts concerning Tony Lock's action—not all the time but particularly when he bowled his faster ball. When facing Lock, Hassett would often call down the pitch: 'Strike 1', 'Strike 2' and so on. However, the Surrey bowler who later gave Yeoman service to Western Australia rarely, if ever, failed to satisfy umpires.

After Hutton unaccountably and sadly ran himself out for 17, Edrich, May and Compton knocked the runs off and there was general rejoicing. Both captains made appropriately graceful speeches and England had recovered the Ashes at home for the first time since 1926 when the late Wilfred Rhodes had played a notable part.

The Test match batting was dominated by Hutton with 55.37, demonstrating again his claim to be in the direct line of J B Hobbs. The top Australian was Hassett at 36.5, followed by Harvey 34.6 and Morris 33.7. In what was a fairly low-scoring series, Arthur's contribution was satisfactory although far below his 1948 performance. It is interesting to note that Australia, though beaten, played the more attractive cricket— 45.6 runs per 100 deliveries received compared with England's 34.6 per 100. The local scribes were impressed with the way that Australians attacked when in difficulty. The young players, Davidson, Archer and Hole particularly, refused to be bogged down, while Lindwall, in the veteran class, more than once demonstrated a frightening ability to tear the attack to shreds when it had seemed to be on top.

At Lord's, the elusive century at last came Arthur's way in the second innings of a match against the Gentlemen. Chasing 253, Morris and Harvey were fittingly together after McDonald and Miller departed. Arthur played in his best style for 126 not out and was highly delighted that his run of fifties and sixties had at last come to an end and with an Australian victory. But his luck didn't last. He was out for 8 against Kent, where the presence of Frank Woolley is almost tangible. The Australians won by an innings and Bill Johnston had 11 wickets for the match.

Arthur missed the match against the South of England and got a third ball duck against Combined Services trying to hit a six. T N Pearce's XI (previously H G Leveson–Gower's side), turned out a Test Eleven against the Australians in the 'Festival Match' at Scarborough. With only three Yorkshiremen, the game had a little more Festival spirit than some corresponding matches of earlier tours, particularly the 1938 engagement when six Yorkshiremen turned out. Yorkshire cricketers generally pay only lip service to Festival matches. They regard all cricket matches as serious affairs, particularly those against 't 'Aussies'.

Richie Benaud made 135 in 110 minutes with eleven sixes and nine fours. With Arthur Morris his opening partner, the pair put on 163, Arthur using his bat as a rapier in scoring 70, while Benaud brandished a broadsword. The 3½ hours were more than enough to knock off the 320 runs required. Earlier Hutton put together his 122nd career century in regal fashion and even time. It would have been a sight for all to enjoy, but it was not enough to prevent an Australian win.

Arthur wound up his tour with a lightning century against the Scots at Paisley. An enthusiastic crowd of 5000 were delighted at the range of strokes on display and cries of 'Hoots mon' assailed the crisp, northern air as Richie Benaud blasted four sixes and eight fours in a score of 89, made in just over the hour. A day lost to the elements prevented a decision, but the Scots performed well with 3–100 in reply to Australia's 9–377. A young man named Chisholm demonstrated a touch of class with 55 not out in the Paisley game, followed by 43 and 41 at Edinburgh a day or two later. The skirl of the pipes, some voodoo bowling by Hassett (3–2) and a curtain of Scotch mist marked the end of proceedings for the 1953 Australians and they headed for home. They'd been away for six months, had lost only one match—the fifth Test—and had endeared themselves to one and all.

Arthur Morris finished seventh in the tour averages (sixth if Bill Johnston's contrived figure of 102 is disregarded). With 1302 runs at 38.29, it was satisfactory if not sensational. He had also met a beautiful girl to whom he would soon be married.

Reflecting recently (on his batting) on the 1953 tour, Arthur confesses to a certain lighthearted approach to his batting, not evident five years previously. The centuries were scarce but the fifties and sixties numerous and mostly compiled in a fashion that brought much pleasure to those who watched. Meeting Valerie Hudson might have had something to do with this approach.

Tyson and Statham Rampant AUSTRALIA 1954–55

a severe case of 'the biter bit'

RETURNING FROM THE TOUR OF ENGLAND, the Australians were glad that the season coming up at home would be a domestic one without the added excitement and strain of a visiting side. This had not happened since the 1948–49 season, again after a long tour of England.

Arthur played in five Sheffield Shield matches plus a Testimonial Match for Lindsay Hassett who had hung his boots up after the tour of England. The little man captained one side and Morris the other, the match being played in Melbourne. Morris was bowled by Miller for 7 in the first innings and fell to Ian Johnson for 52 in the second.

He made 171 in Brisbane against Queensland and followed this with 126 and 9 in Adelaide against South Australia. Moving on to Melbourne, Jack Hill had him leg before for 70 and he was not out 27 in the second innings. Playing Queensland in Sydney, his run of good scores ended with 19, caught at the wicket from Ron Archer's bowling. After the Testimonial Match referred to earlier, he played against Victoria in Sydney but was out for 5 and 1. Thanks to the two early centuries, his average of 54.11 from 487 runs was his best since the 1950–51 season.

With the winter break, thoughts were starting to focus on the

129

'Ashes' series against England in the following season. Hassett's retirement left a question mark over the captaincy and the names of Morris, Miller and Ian Johnson were before the selectors. Both Morris and Miller had skippered New South Wales and Ian Johnson had inherited Lindsay Hassett's mantle for Victoria. With Lindwall, Miller and Johnston now into their thirties, the merits of young players Davidson, Archer and Benaud were prominent in selectors' minds. It was apparent that England's star was rising and that a severe battle could be anticipated. With Len Hutton captain, a professional and a Yorkshireman, no easy runs or wickets could be expected. Young players like May, Graveney and Colin Cowdrey had all demonstrated class and England had now almost an embarrassment of effective fast bowlers in Trueman, Tyson and Statham to support the proven Alec Bedser.

The party chosen for the tour was:

HUTTON L	(CAPTAIN)	YORKSHIRE
MAY P B H	(VICE-CAPTAIN	SURREY
APPLEYARD R		
WARDLE J		YORKSHIRE
WILSON J W		
BAILEY T E		ESSEX
BEDSER A V		
LOADER P J		SURREY
COMPTON D C S		
EDRICH W J		MIDDLESEX
ANDREW K V		
TYSON F H		NORTHAMPTON
COWDREY M C		
EVANS T G		KENT
McCONNON J E		GLAMORGAN
GRAVENEY T W		GLOUCESTERSHIRE
SIMPSON R T		NOTTINGHAMSHIRE
STATHAM J B		LANCASHIRE

Most surprising was the omission of Lock and Laker who had wrecked Australia's batting 18 months previously and the preference of Peter Loader to Trueman as the third pace bowler.

Morris and Miller had shared the captaincy of the New South Wales' side, but Morris had so far been preferred as vice-captain of the national side and his appointment in Hassett's place was widely canvassed. In the event, the honour went to Ian Johnson, not a popular choice in NSW where traditional interstate rivalries predictably surfaced. It was felt that Johnson, who had not been considered good enough to gain selection in the 1953 touring party, had doubtful claims to the captaincy 18 months later. Playing in four Tests, Johnson, with the help of four not outs, headed the batting averages with 58 and was second in the bowling with 12 wickets at 20.25.

Arthur Morris started the season modestly with scores of 27 and 26 in the State game against Queensland. He did not play again until the Englishmen reached Sydney. Hutton had shown good form in Adelaide against South Australia with 37 and 98, and Tyson bowled fast, if a little erratically, claiming 6 wickets. The match against an Australian XI in Melbourne was spoilt by rain and did not help the selectors of either side greatly, except that Ian Johnson probably clinched his appointment as captain for the Tests, taking 6–66. The match was drawn.

Against NSW, Hutton scored heavily in both innings with 102 and 87. Miller led NSW and, winning the toss, sent the MCC in to bat, a habit becoming fairly common in Australian cricket, and turning upside down established practice except in the case of rain-damaged wickets. Hutton watched impassively while Edrich, Simpson, May and Wilson were all out with only 38 runs on the board against some fairly run-of-the-mill bowling. Then Cowdrey joined his captain in a fine stand of 163 in even time. Hutton batted with his expected calm mastery, but most interest centred on the 22-year-old Colin Cowdrey. Many voted him, on this showing, the best post-war batsman seen from England. His timing, placement and defence were faultless. Added to this he displayed equanimity in a difficult situation, which suggested a fine temperament. Batting with his captain, arguably the world's most accomplished player, this innings would have been of considerable value not only for the runs scored but as a grounding for the future. Apart from Hutton and Cowdrey, the score book made dismal reading indeed, only Godfrey Evans reaching double figures. The total of 252 was more an example of poor batsmanship than inspired captaincy on Miller's part. The home side's fielding was first class. Bob Simpson took three catches at first slip, Bill Watson two more at second slip.

Coming in late in the day, Morris attacked Alec Bedser, at once seeking to establish authority over the great bowler. He took 14 from the first over, the big man being a trifle off line and uncertain in length. New South Wales went in at 0–19 next morning, and Bedser soon had Arthur from a mistimed drive into the covers. No doubt Bedser, who had been on the sick list with shingles virtually since the team's arrival, derived some satisfaction at having drawn early blood from his old adversary. Miller and Bill Watson played well to lift the side and, despite some disappointing efforts by players with Test match aspirations, the innings closed at a respectable 382. England, batting again, would have fared lamentably but for the two heroes of the first innings. Hutton played in his habitual studious style for 87 and young Cowdrey made another century, the first Englishman to do the double against an Australian State since Andy Sandham in 1924–25. His batting impressed everyone and it seemed that a potential champion was waiting to make his entry onto the Test match stage. Scoring 327, England left NSW 198 to win and there was simply insufficient time. Morris did not bat in the second innings. England had saved the game in a far from impressive exhibition which, apart from Cowdrey's batting and Bedser's return to something like his best form, left quite a few question marks over the composition of the Test side.

As it happened, Cowdrey came back to earth with a thud in the game against Queensland, the curtain raiser for the Test match in Brisbane. He opened in both innings with Reg Simpson and was out caught at the wicket by Wally Grout off Lindwall for 4, and in the second innings clean bowled by Ron Archer for the minimum. The England batting was again patchy, with two or three holding it together in both innings while the others only added to the troubles of Hutton, watching from the pavilion. Simpson, Bailey, May and Compton (twice) all got runs. Lindwall's bowling impressed and he was clearly certain to be a force in the series despite advancing years. Bedser, too, now almost completely recovered from his illness, sent down thirty-one overs for 56 runs and two wickets. Time ran out before a decision could be reached.

England entered the Test match minus the inspiring presence of Godfrey Evans behind the stumps and without a spin bowler. The attack comprised Tyson, Statham, Bedser and Bailey.

Arthur remembers feeling some slight concern at facing Tyson again after his painful experience the previous year at Northampton. The wicket for the State match just concluded had been lively and most felt that the Test wicket might be similar. This may have been a factor in Hutton's otherwise inexplicable decision to send Australia in. Morris had similar misgivings and his feelings as he awaited Tyson's arrival at the bowling crease from somewhere almost within sight of the Brisbane City Hall were a little apprehensive. The American comedian, W C Fields, left instructions that his tombstone was to be inscribed, 'All in all I'd rather be in Philadelphia'. Arthur felt much the same—not necessarily Philadelphia but anywhere other than the 'Gabba. As things turned out, the pitch was somnolent and Hutton's decision proved to be a disaster.

After only an hour of play, Denis Compton crashed into the fence and broke a bone in his hand. Morris was in attacking mood and struck a Bedser no-ball for six. The two 'friendly rivals' allowed themselves a brief chuckle as the ball was returned. He and Les Favell put on 51 before Favell, hooking but mis-timing, got a touch to a Statham bouncer and was caught at leg slip by Cowdrey. Keith Miller, batting in ominously good touch, was unlucky to chop a Bailey delivery on to his stumps after adding 72 with Morris. The latter, who had kept pace with Miller, slowed down upon his dismissal and, with Harvey completely out of touch, the score crawled to 142 at the tea adjournment. Bedser was then unlucky to have Morris dropped by Bailey at deep square leg—a simple catch. Any chuckling after this escape was confined to the batsmen.

The two left-handers proceeded with growing confidence there-after, both short of batting practice but not lacking in determination, and they were together at the close, Morris bruised but unbowed on 82 after five hours, Harvey on 41 scored in more than two hours. With the total 2–208, Hutton was no doubt undertaking a thorough reap-praisal of his decision to field. Australia's slow scoring should be judged on overs bowled—only 58 eight ball overs in five hours.

Next morning Morris was more readily identifiable as Morris and runs came at a rapid rate. A couple of barely possible dropped catches added to England's woes and Bailey resorted to leg theory until hit for six by Arthur, over square leg. At lunch Arthur was 138, clearly outs-coring a still struggling Harvey—Morris 56 in the morning's play com-pared with Harvey's 35.

Arthur Morris was out soon after lunch for 153 made in just seven hours and on the morning's evidence was back in his best form. He suffered a severe bruising from the battering the fast bowlers handed out in this innings, but he and Harvey had added 202 runs for the third wicket. Thereafter, it was uphill all the way for England. Everybody got a few except Ron Archer and there were some unflattering figures among the bowlers in the total of 8–601 (declared). Bedser had 1–131, Statham 2–123, Tyson 1–160, Bailey 3–140. The over rate was appall-ingly slow, with pace bowlers operating continuously, and Tyson, in particular, attacking from somewhere near the sightboard. It must be noted with regret that Hutton consciously slowed this game, and those that followed, by frequent meticulous field placements and alterations. It seemed too, that the bowlers were under instruction to keep the brakes on, and to attack the leg stump. There was at this time no rule restricting the number of fieldsmen behind square leg to two.

With Compton injured, the England situation was far from a happy one as Hutton and Simpson walked out to open the innings after seven sessions in the field. Hutton fell cheaply in both innings, once to Lind-wall, the other time to Miller. Cowdrey played well for 40 in the first innings and, with the tenacious Bailey, gave a modicum of spine to his side's performance. Edrich batted bravely in the second innings and May gave fleeting glimpses of his class. The less said about the others the better. All the Australian bowlers participated in the demolition with Lindwall being perhaps the best. Making due allowances for Hutton's initial error in electing to field, and Compton's injury, the England cricket was sub-standard for the most part and lacking in backbone. It would have pained many who'd gone before. Bedser was still a little short of a gallop although he was unlucky to have several catches dropped. There was some fine batting by the Australians, Morris and Harvey groping their way to top form after uncertain beginnings and Miller's 49 being as good as had been seen from him for some time.

The win by an innings and 154 runs was good reason for some self-congratulation. Perhaps it was fitting that rejoicing should be general because there was to be a notable absence of euphoria from this time on. For England, subsequent events suggest that the lessons were well earned and applied because they were not to know any later defeat.

'The second Test in Sydney was a low-scoring game which generated much excitement and some fine individual efforts on a lively and variable pitch. It saw the coming to maturity of England's finest young batsmen since World War II in May and Cowdrey and the flowering of a pair of lethal fast bowlers in Tyson and Statham. All four were under 25 years of age. Arthur Morris recalls that the pitch was green and lively at one end and tended to keep low at the other. Ian Johnson and Keith Miller were unavailable due to injury so that Arthur inherited the captaincy. His evaluation of the two-paced appearance of the pitch prompted him to 'invite' the Englishmen to bat first despite Hutton's disastrous Brisbane experience. The chief selection surprise was the dropping of Bedser, who learned of his omission only when he perused the team list in the dressing room just before the match. The 'Lion of Surrey' did not appreciate this lack of sensitivity in his captain and it would certainly seem that courtesy might have dictated a more considerate approach to one who had borne England's bowling since the war almost singlehanded. Simpson was the other one omitted and, after playing without a spinner in Brisbane, England brought in two—Appleyard and Wardle. The opening batsmen's duties were to be taken over by Bailey who, in the event, failed twice. Compton, still injured, was replaced by Graveney. For Australia, an injured Miller was replaced by Jim Burke and Davidson came in for Ian Johnson.

After Lindwall despatched Bailey for nought, Hutton went on his 'calm, sequestered way' as the poet Gray has it, until he was brilliantly caught at backward square leg from an authentic clip off the meat of the bat that had four runs written all over it. Alan Davidson, a natural left-hander, moved initially to the left, corrected himself and dived to the right, catching the ball an inch from the ground. Hutton, bemused and unbelieving, departed the scene in sorrow.

Thereafter the batting caused one to ponder whether this was a Test match or an engagement between Engonia and Snake Gully into which one had strayed. The innings and, as things turned out, the loss of the game, was saved by some intelligent tail-end use of the long handle by Johnny Wardle who top scored with 35. Last man Statham put some of his more illustrious colleagues to shame with 14 not out in a brave stand of 43 for the last wicket. The innings ended at 154.

Arthur Morris opened with Favell and was unlucky to get a brute of a delivery in the day's last over from Bailey. It rose sharply to his armpit. Arthur tried to 'kill' it by letting go of the bat with his right hand but the ball dollied to Hutton at leg slip. The score was 18. Next day provided some fascinating cricket. Trevor Bailey will remember his spell in the afternoon with pleasure until his life's end. He attacked the off stump, moved the ball a little each way and had both Burke and Les Favell well taken by Graveney in the gully. This gave Bailey the first three wickets and the gaping hole in the batting was soon enlarged by some fierce bowling from Tyson and Statham. The former had shortened his run and was a fearsome sight—quite easily the fastest bowling the Australians had encountered since the war and possibly as long ago as Larwood. Statham, coming in from the northern end into the southerly, was accurate and always penetrative so that the batsmen had no let up—a unique experience for Australian batsmen in those days. The two fast bowlers got six of the last seven wickets to fall, the deserving Bailey winning the other. Graeme Hole, with his high back lift, had his bat still held aloft as a Tyson thunderbolt crashed into the stumps. Of the Australians, Burke had been solid in making 44, and Ron Archer hit bravely lower down the list. But it was painfully apparent that Australia was going to have a measure of trouble from Messrs Tyson and Statham. With 228, Australia were 74 ahead and this would have been sufficient but for some fine batting by England's two young hopes, May and Cowdrey. Hutton, playing well, unaccountably failed to get across when trying to drive Bill Johnston and was well taken by Benaud in the gully. Graveney was quickly out but there was no further joy for Australia until 5pm when Cowdrey lofted a drive straight to Archer off Benaud's bowling. At 4–171, England were 97 ahead and Bill Edrich added another 50-odd with May, who was 98 not out at the close. He went to a well earned century but fell soon after to Lindwall with the new ball. Lindwall then hit Tyson a severe blow on the back of the head, sending him to hospital for x-rays, which showed no damage. Indeed, any damage caused probably came Australia's way, the blow raising Tyson's ire and making him very anxious to get at them in the second innings.

Statham again revealed batting skills previously unnoticed in making 25, and the innings, which appeared to be on the rocks when May and Edrich left, struggled on to a respectable 296. Lindwall, Archer and Johnston all took three wickets. Australia now needed 223 to win, a task most thought well within their capacity. Tyson and Statham thought otherwise. Arthur was leg before to the industrious Statham who, with Tyson, decimated the Australian batting. Harvey was the splendid exception. His 92 not out does not stand out as world-beating, but Harvey himself would rate the innings well ahead of many more prolific efforts. Hole's dismissal was a repeat of his first innings' experience, and Burke suffered a similar fate. With the score at 9–145, Bill Johnston joined Harvey who had been a pained witness of some earlier dissmissals. The two added 39 in an exciting partnership which some optimists hoped might continue until the runs were knocked off. There was some comedy in Johnston's innings but Harvey's was all class. He played the two fast bowlers with comparative ease and without making a false stroke, and at no stage looked likely to lose his wicket. It was certainly not his fault that England won by 38 runs. The Australians considered this wicket slow at one end and lively at the other and unsuitable for a Test match.

Arthur Morris considers that Tyson bowled faster in this match than anyone he'd encountered. He was certainly an awesome sight—a powerfully built man with a high arm action and a very aggressive attitude. His general appearance, build and dislike of batsmen were a little reminiscent of O'Reilly. His temper in this Sydney game had probably not been improved by the smack on the head he'd received from Lindwall a day or two earlier. Brian Statham, not so ferocious, but persistent, accurate and always making the batsman play at the ball, was the perfect foil for Tyson. Statham's lot was to bowl into the wind but this reduced neither his effectiveness nor spirit. Tyson's great season was just beginning and seemed to be related, in large measure, to the shortening of his run. This gave him greater rhythm, greater accuracy and was less tiring. He was never as effective after this Australian summer and, on his return in 1958, was far less threatening. Statham, of course, went on to take 252 Test wickets at 24.82. This compares with Tyson's 76 at 18.56, Trueman's 307 at 21.57 and John Snow's 202 at 26.67.

Arthur played for New South Wales against Victoria in Melbourne before the third Test which was due to start there on New Year's Eve. He had a good match with 28 and 78 and was satisfied with his form. The Australians who gathered at the MCG for the next encounter were, no doubt, a little thoughtful at the dramatic reversal of form shown by England in the Sydney match, after their Brisbane effort. Miller came back for Jim Burke, who could consider himself a little hardly done by, Ian Johnson resumed the captaincy and Davidson had to make way for him. Langley had an eye injury and was replaced by Len Maddocks.

For England, Compton returned at Graveney's expense and Bedser, whose star seemed sadly to be setting, was again omitted. In this remarkable match, watched by more than 300 000 people over five days, the Melbourne wicket presented problems to the batsmen of both sides—problems not at all convincingly dealt with except by Cowdrey in the first innings and May in the second. Top scorer for Australia in either innings was Maddocks with 47. Arthur Morris's memories of the pitch are tinged with mingled horror and amazement. He says that some of the cracks were so wide, that had Lindsay Hassett still been playing, he could have disappeared for ever down one of them. Arthur fell twice to Tyson for 3 and 4. The two fast bowlers resumed where they'd left off in Sydney, Tyson having 9 wickets and Statham 7 for the match. Cowdrey, who might well have been unnerved by the dismissal in quick succession of Hutton, Edrich and May, again showed both class and temperament in scoring 102 out of his side's 191 in what was considered one of the finest innings seen at the MCG. The Melbourne crowd of 63,814 gave him a lengthy standing ovation as he left the ground after losing his wicket to a freakish delivery from Ian Johnson which pitched wide of the off stump and turned almost at right angles. Miller's early bowling had been electrifying and at lunch his figures were 9 overs 8 maidens 5 runs 3 wickets.

When Australia batted, the over rate became funereal, with Tyson and Statham both fielding on the boundary when not bowling. This resulted in lengthy delays as each returned to the bowling crease before walking with measured tread to his bowling mark. Hutton's frequent and meticulous field changes and placements again slowed the game.

Apart from Harvey and Maddocks, the Australians were guilty of unconvincing batting on a pitch now decidedly variable in both bounce and pace against bowling that was consistently and disturbingly fast and on the spot. Perhaps 231 could have been regarded as reasonable, having regard to the pitch, if England had collapsed in its second innings on a track which was a day older. But they applied themselves and, with Hutton holding on although far from comfortable, and May batting with style and authority for 91, the others managed enough to lift the side's total to 279, a lead of 239.

Australia's batting in their last three innings defied belief. Most people thought that this Melbourne innings would put any doubts to rest and that 'the Poms' would get a thrashing. Arthur Morris was at the wicket for thirty-six minutes in making 4 and Favell top scored with 30. The less said about the others the better. The pitch must accept some blame—many deliveries kept low, particularly when the ball hit the edge of one of the cracks (or craters?) and Messrs Tyson and Statham, all fired up and never an easy proposition, were lethal. But there was some very indifferent batting, lacking both in spirit and technique. The last eight wickets fell for 34 runs and Tyson finished with 7–27 from

12.3 overs. Statham was, as ever, tidy and persistent and gave the batsmen no respite. The Australians were out for 111, England won by 128 runs, and the fate of the Ashes was now in the melting pot.

Poor Arthur Morris! Nothing was going well for him at this stage. Turning out for New South Wales against Victoria in Sydney, he was out for a duck to a lively bowler named John Power. This young man bounced Keith Miller four times in succession in the last over before lunch in this match. Miller, somewhat discomfited, very deliberately walked down the wicket after bouncer number two and ostentatiously patted the pitch in the vicinity of where Power completed his follow-through. The feeling in the middle couldn't be mistaken and Power let him have a couple more. The luncheon adjournment terminated what might otherwise have produced an interesting passage of play.

England were now riding high. They walloped Tasmania and South Australia, Cowdrey, Compton, May, Graveney and Hutton all turning in some splendid batting in one or other of the three games.

There had been some criticism of Morris's batting to this point, but everyone was surprised, many outraged, when he was dropped. He'd always scored well at Adelaide and his class had been established in many a Test match. After some backing and filling, and injury to Lindwall, the selectors finally discarded Favell (on his own midden) and reinstated Arthur, to open with Colin McDonald. England had few problems, the only criticism being the retention of Bill Edrich for Graveney. The latter was now in something like his best form, but then Edrich was always a sturdy performer and could also bowl a bit. This latter attribute appeared hardly relevant considering the recent quality of the opposition's batting.

On a hot day, Australia won the toss and batted first. The heat curtailed lengthy operations by Tyson and Statham and the Australians reached 51 by lunch without loss—Morris 22, McDonald 25. Neither had appeared in difficulty and the runs gathered appeared reasonable enough having regard to the poor over-rate. Arthur was in fairly good touch and it appeared his run of outs might have ended. But Statham, rejuvenated and refreshed after lunch, unsettled him with a good over and Tyson reaped the benefit when Arthur got a sliver of glove on a ball from which he tried to withdraw the bat, to be caught by Evans.

For a side that needed a win in this match if the Ashes were to be regained, the batting that followed was disappointing and without purpose. Burke and McDonald hung about on the defensive until Harvey and Miller put some life into the innings later in the afternoon, although both were far from their best. Then Benaud, a punishing player in Shield cricket, dawdled for 75 minutes accumulating 15 runs. Many possible singles went begging and the day's play over 300 minutes yielded only 161 runs. This poor rate must again be related to the number of overs bowled—58, a quota which makes the present West Indies team look almost lively. The best feature of the cricket was Evans's work behind the stumps, which confirmed him as easily the best wicket-keeper in the business. Wickets fell at regular intervals in wearisome succession until Ian Johnson, coming in second-last, joined Maddocks. These two put their better qualified colleagues to shame. They added 92 in even time, Maddocks embellishing his display by several splendid strokes including an off-drive from Statham's bowling which would have adorned any match, at any time. When Johnson left, Maddocks was run out, trying to shield his partner Bill Johnston from the strike—a doubtful compliment to the man who'd headed the 1953 averages? The 323 total was respectable, if not sensational.

England's batting for the remaining 90 minutes was solid rather than spectacular but they went in with 57 runs on the board without losing a wicket. Next day Hutton passed 50 for the first time in the series but saw May brilliantly caught at slip by Archer. Ian Johnson bowled accurately without luck and completed 18 overs while conceding only 24 runs. He had troubled Hutton in previous seasons and kept him well contained again on this occasion. The batting was slow and the crowd restless and even the advent of Compton to join Cowdrey provided no relief. Hutton was caught for 80 in 270 minutes. The third day's play ended with England 3–230, which boiled down to 173 runs in the day, the difference being that the Australians bowled 81 overs compared with England's 58 on the first day.

Next morning saw both Compton and Cowdrey quickly departing. Evans hit lustily for 37 in even time and Wardle followed suit when he joined the tenacious Bailey—with all his faults, an extremely useful and intelligent Test match cricketer. The innings ended in mid-afternoon, and in the forty minutes before tea, Arthur Morris batted well until he managed to crack Cowdrey accidentally in the eye. A cut off Appleyard's bowling hit a rough patch and reared up catching the fieldsman a nasty blow which necessitated his retirement for some repair work. Arthur was out a couple of balls later when he misjudged Appleyard's flight and was caught and bowled for 16. Appleyard was theoretically an off-spin bowler but relied more on changes of pace and length which, with unusual bounce, presented problems to batsmen. He was a very effective bowler at all levels of the game but suffered from bad health during his career which was as a result unfortunately shortened. After seeing Morris off in this innings, he quickly accounted for Burke and Harvey, the latter trying to swing a good length ball to leg to be bowled. The dyke was well and truly breached now and next day saw the Australians engulfed in the flood. Statham skittled McDonald and Miller in quick succession and none of the others proved difficult to dislodge. Appleyard had 3–13 from 12 overs, and Tyson and Statham had three each as well in the total of 111. The Australian batting had crumbled once more against a purposeful, unrelenting attack. Only 94 runs were required for England to win the rubber and the series.

Keith Miller bowled like a man possessed to send Hutton, Edrich and Cowdrey back with only 18 runs on the board. Then, to show his versatility and hurt pride, he hurled himself full length at extra cover to catch Peter May off Johnston. Bailey was leg before to Johnston and the fifth wicket fell at 90. Evans and Compton sealed the match for England. Since Brisbane, which in retrospect appeared an aberration, the home side had gradually crumbled while their opponents went from strength to strength. This was England's first Ashes series victory in Australia since Douglas Jardine stirred things up in the 1932–33 'Body-line' series.

Since the Brisbane Test, Arthur Morris had batted six times for 70 runs. On this performance he might be considered to have been a trifle lucky to be selected to tour the West Indies. In the return match for New South Wales against England, he may well have recovered his lost touch but unfortunately he had to withdraw due to the after-effects of vaccination. His absence from this game was no doubt important in the selectors' minds when they omitted him from the final Test match.

The State game, as it happened, saw the home team running out winners by 45 runs. There were no big scores but most of those engaged, on both sides, had a measure of success. It gave much pleasure to see Bedser back among the wickets, with 5 in the first innings and a couple in the second. The New South Wales openers, Ron Briggs and Burke, performed indifferently—Briggs got a pair and Burke 0 and 62. Morris might have bettered these figures substantially had he played, and possibly hung on to his Test spot.

Australia did little to recover lost prestige in the Sydney Test and the rain-shortened match gave England a moral victory. Tom Graveney, opening the innings, at last showed his true form, with 111 in 166 minutes of batting which was probably the best seen on either side during the tour. He hit 14 fours and, with May, added 182 in his 166 minutes at the crease. The match was drawn.

It had been a bad season for Australian cricket, the worst, said Bill O'Reilly, since 1912 in England. The Brisbane total of 600, in retrospect, did more harm than good in that it gave the Australians a mistaken sense of their superiority over England's bowlers. In subsequent games, they were brutally disillusioned. In six innings since Brisbane, as noted, Morris added 70 runs to his 153 in that Test match. That gave him an average of 31.85 which placed him still fairly high in the averages of recognised batsmen who had played a significant number of innings. Neil Harvey, with 354 at 44.25, had the best record, and his 92 not out at Sydney was among the three best innings of the series.

With a tour of the West Indies on top of them (the first ever by an Australian team), the selectors had an unenviable task in selecting a side. The terrain and conditions were unknown, crowds, accommodation, distances could only be gleaned at second-hand from the experience of other countries who had toured. The cry for an infusion of youth was understandable, but on the other hand it would have been foolhardy to discard players of proven value in new conditions. Arthur Morris was such a player. He'd scored centuries on his first appearance in both England and South Africa as well as his maiden effort of two centuries in first-class cricket at home. Despite some doubts regarding his form in the season just passed, he was a batsman of universally admitted class and he was only 33 years old. These factors would have carried weight in team selection.

In the

Caribbean

1955

Walcott's magnificence

FOLLOWING THEIR DRUBBING by Hutton's 1954–55 England team, featuring the fire and fury of Tyson and Statham, Australian cricketers were looking forward to a more tranquil time in early 1955 in the Caribbean against the West Indies. In the way of speed bowlers, little was known of anyone of express pace. Certain it was that there wouldn't be any Tysons or Stathams around. In 1955 this was the reality of things. How times change! Our present crowd of cricketers would gladly put the clock back and subject themselves to the wiles of Valentine and Ramadhin if by doing so they would be divested of Curtly Ambrose and Co. As it turned out, there were no express bowlers of class and the standard encountered generally was mediocre. Ramadhin and Valentine had little success and the Australians scored heavily, with Neil Harvey again the scourge of all bowlers.

There was considerable interest in the tour, mainly because it would be the first occasion in which an Australian side had played the West Indies in their homeland. They did not quite know what to expect in the way of wickets, umpires, or crowds or indeed the players they would encounter. Nor did they imagine that Clyde Walcott, the least effective of the '3 Ws' in Australia in 1951–52, would tear their bowlers to shreds and make five centuries in the series—an unheard of achievement and one which had eluded even the great Bradman. The other significant occurrence was the appearance on the international scene of one who was, and still is regarded as the greatest all-round cricketer ever. Garfield Sobers had appeared in the match against the touring England side in the final Test of the 1953–54 series at Kingston. In that game he took 4–75 in England's first innings of 414.

In the series now approaching, he was to show early signs of his genius as batsman, multi-talented bowler and cat-like close-in fieldsman.

Although in the number of matches arranged it would be a shortish tour, climatic conditions and the distances between venues suggested to the selectors, Messrs Bradman, Don Seddon and Jack Ryder, that a 16-man side was desirable. Those selected were:

JOHNSON I W	VIC	CAPTAIN
MILLER K R	NSW	VICE-CAPTAIN
ARCHER R G	QLD	
BENAUD R	NSW	
BURGE P J P	QLD	
DAVIDSON A K	NSW	
FAVELL L E	SA	
HARVEY R N	VIC	
HILL J C	VIC	
JOHNSTON W A	VIC	
LANGLEY G R A	SA	
LINDWALL R R	NSW	
McDONALD C C	VIC	
MADDOCKS L V	VIC	
MORRIS A R	NSW	
WATSON W J	NSW	

As always, there was criticism. Bill O'Reilly dubbed the selectors 'The Three Unwise Men of Cricket', and Mailey and Fingleton were also censorious. The main bone of contention was the appointment of Ian Johnson as captain. The preference of Johnson over Miller and Morris had been criticised in 1954–55 when he led Australia in four Tests against England. In that series, with the aid of four 'not outs', he'd headed the batting averages and was second in the bowling averages with twelve wickets at 20.25. As things turned out, the choice of Ian Johnson and Miller as the two leaders with Morris the third selector proved a singularly happy one. Their easy relationship with the people of the Caribbean, both players and spectators, was in sharp contrast to the stiff-collared approach of the Englishmen the previous season.

The side's batsmen were: Morris, Harvey, McDonald, Burge, Favell and Watson. Outright bowlers were: Johnston, Hill, Lindwall, who would be well supported by all-rounders Miller, Davidson, Benaud, Ian Johnson and Archer. Langley and Maddocks were the two wicket-keepers. The absence of Hole and Jim Burke was lamented, but Burge and Billy Watson had good home performances to support their inclusion.

Ian Johnson on arrival in Jamaica did an interview on the local radio station. One of the questions asked was: 'Do you think that old cricketers Stan McCabe, Bill O'Reilly and Jack Fingleton are helping young Australians?' Johnson was reported as replying: 'McCabe would like to but present day Australians are unanimously of the opinion that neither Fingleton nor O'Reilly has written during the past season one constructive word about the game.' If this account is true, it probably explains Bill O'Reilly's lukewarm opinion of Ian Johnson. All three accused are now dead, so it's a little hard to assess the validity of the statement.

Generally the press shared the public's view of the senior Australian players, namely that they were most helpful and cooperative.

There was to be only one lead-up match before the first Test match and that was to be at Melbourne Park, Kingston, against a Jamaican side.

Arthur Morris got away to a flying start and, after being missed when 32, he went on to score 157, his best effort since the first Test against England, in Brisbane in late 1954 when he'd made 153. He came to his century in just three hours; the whole innings occupied just over four hours and included twenty-three fours and one six. He was understandably feeling some relief at not being confronted by Tyson and Statham, and the local press was already acknowledging that as a No 1 he was a formidable proposition.

Morris now had the unusual distinction of having made a century in his initial first-class match in four countries—Australia, England, South Africa and West Indies. He was elated at his century and saw it as a welcome 'come back' performance following his poor run of scores at home in the season just ended.

For the locals, the dazzling Collie Smith made 169 in quick time and Jamaica, with 474, headed the Australians' 453. R S Whitington wrote that he thought he was witnessing the genuine birth of another Bradman. We've heard this accolade bestowed on a few players, but the early promise has never been fulfilled, nor is it likely to be. As for Collie Smith, he gave much pleasure to many people, but his Test match average of 31.6 says it all. He bowled a bit as well, taking Morris's wicket in this innings, and was a cheerful and well-loved man whose death following a car accident in 1959 saddened many. Gary Sobers was also involved in the accident but escaped with minor injuries.

Australia's second innings of 9–319 included 22 by Morris. The match was drawn. The Test match in Jamaica followed closely upon the lead-up game. Ian Johnson won the toss and the Australians, batting first, scored heavily. Arthur opened with Colin McDonald and had reached 42 at lunch with the score at 82. The pair went on to 102 before Arthur was out leg before to Valentine for 65. There was a nearly impossible chance when he was on 38, but otherwise his innings was in his best opening style and the two had seen the side off to a very satisfactory start. Frank King was a lively bowler who tended to over-exploit the bumper. Perhaps he set the stage for future years and future players. Harvey and Miller both scored centuries in the Australian total of 9–515. The home team's bowling was completely collared and Denis Atkinson the captain resorted to Clyde Walcott, usually the wicket-keeper, to put his arm over. Curiously, he finished with the best figures of 3–50, which was a commendable effort for a man from whom so much was expected in his other roles.

Indeed, Walcott held the batting together when the West Indies batted, hitting powerfully after the others crumbled before the many-faceted art of Ray Lindwall, then in his 34th year. Lindwall had reduced his speed but had lost little of his earlier effectiveness—like Lillee 25 years later, he had an extensive repertoire of inswingers and outswingers, leg cutters and yorkers with subtle variations in pace and length. In this innings he took 4–61 and forced the home team to follow on. Batting again, Collie Smith demonstrated that his earlier century against Australia was no fluke, his 104 including fourteen fours and occupying 200 minutes. His effort availed little other than to force the Australians to bat again to knock off the 20 runs required to win. Arthur Morris opened with Len Maddocks but did not trouble the scorers greatly, being brilliantly caught at leg slip for 1. The Australians won by 9 wickets. Keith Miller had a good match with 147 and 3–62 in the home side's second innings of 275.

The Australians flew from Kingston, Jamaica, to Port of Spain on the island of Trinidad, a distance of about 2000 kilometres, no mean flight forty-odd years ago. Two games were scheduled—one against the provincial team with the second Test match following closely. The island's most famous cricketing son was Learie Constantine, who was finally elevated to the peerage by the British Government in recognition of his services to cricket, the law, government and a few other matters, notably of a literary and welfare nature. Constantine died in 1971. Gerry Gomez, Jeff Stollmeyer and Sonny Ramadhin are the island's other notable cricketing progeny. Ramadhin absented himself from the provincial game, no doubt to keep secret for the Test match whatever it was he still had up his sleeve.

Johnson and Miller were laid aside due to illness and Morris led the Australians in the provincial game. Ray Lindwall, bowling with much of his old life and fire, and mixing his deliveries, completely bewildered the locals to take 6–41 in the island's first innings. In reply, the Australians were restricted to a modest 299 of which Favell made 71. Morris had opened the batting with him and was a little slow responding to his partner's call, to be thrown out when going along nicely at 21. The Trinidadians gave the Australians a leather-hunting in their second innings. Jeff Stollmeyer, an elegant opening batsman who skippered the national side on several occasions, scored 95 and Hammond Furlonge, a right-handed opener with a penchant for the hook, which he applied several times to Lindwall, was 150 not out when the innings was closed at 4–290. This effort, following 57 in the first innings, was sufficient to earn him a spot in the Test match. The game, destined for a draw, petered out with some of the lower order players getting some batting practice in Australia's second innings. The ball used in this match was hand stitched and of the type usually used on matting wickets. It seemed harder than usual and the Australians viewed it with some caution, particularly in the catching department, several chances going to ground. Inevitably R S Whitington, a hard man to please, concluded that they were 'funking' the chances. One wonders what he'd have said had Lindwall or Morris broken a finger in attempting a difficult catch on the eve of a Test match.

The Trinidad Test match provided a feast for those who like to see the bat exert complete dominance over the ball. No fewer than six centuries were scored, three to each side, and joy for the bowlers, particularly the West Indians, was in short supply. West Indies batted first and the Australians were treated to some high-class batting from Weekes and Walcott. It was the first occasion on which Everton Weekes had demonstrated the class for which he had been widely acclaimed, except in Australia. He hit seventeen fours and one six in his 139 and, with Walcott, completely subdued the Australian attack. However there wasn't much support from the other players and after such a long partnership, the total of 382 was disappointing. The mighty Lindwall took 6–95 and Richie Benaud 3–44. Morris and McDonald broke the previous best opening partnership for Australia against the West Indies of 173 and went on to 191 when McDonald left. Arthur Morris was uncharacteristically slow early in his innings of 111. He was obviously feeling his way into top form and had a bruised ankle to boot. The second half of his knock was played in his usual style with strokes around the wicket. He took just over five hours for his 111 and was out pulling a short ball from Butler hard to mid-wicket to King, who emerged from a spell of wool-gathering in time to extend a hand into which the ball hurtled and stuck. Neil Harvey made another century and the glut of runs continued, with Archer hitting strongly for 84 and Ian Johnson contributing 66 before he mercifully closed the innings at 9–600.

Batting again, the Weekes–Walcott act was on view once more, the former being 87 not out when rain terminated play at 4–273. Walcott made his second century of the match and joined a very select and restricted band of Test cricketers, including Arthur Morris, who have done this. Australia must have had a reasonable chance of winning this match but for the rain. However, with Weekes still there and the home team 55 runs ahead, it was by no means certain.

The flying distance between Trinidad and Guyana and Barbados is far less than the long Kingston–Trinidad flight and this enabled the second and third Tests to be played close together after the Australians visited Guyana—Morris did not play in this match. Barbados is the home of the greatest number of West Indies champions and, for its small size, the richness and diversity of talent is remarkable. A quick tally reveals at least twenty who have played a significant number of Tests for the West Indies and at least eleven of these, including 'the three Ws' are either in the 'very good' or 'champion' class.

The third Test was played at Georgetown, British Guyana, and was won convincingly by the Australians by eight wickets. To every-body's surprise, not least the Australians, Valentine was dropped as was first Test century-maker Collie Smith. Although the wicket was good, the match was one of low scores with the bowlers very much on top. Batting first, the West Indies could only muster 182, of which Everton Weekes made 81. Richie Benaud took 4–15, including three wickets (Weekes, Norman Marshall and Ramadhin) in four balls. His four wickets, in fact, came from 3.5 overs. The Australians fared rather better after a solid opening stand of 71 by Morris and McDonald. Arthur was out, hooking again, and caught in the outfield by Sobers off the bowling of Atkinson. The hook was proving Arthur's undoing at times but, like McCabe, the stroke yielded him plenty of runs and was a notable characteristic of his batting. In this innings, he made 44 and McDonald 61. The other recognised batsmen fared poorly, but Benaud lent some respectability to the innings with a typically aggressive 68. With the wicket beginning to crumble and the side lacking the batting skills of Bill Johnston who was injured, the total of 257 could be considered adequate. And so it proved. Despite a fine partnership of 125 between Worrell (56) and Walcott, who surprisingly only made 73 on this occasion, the home side was out for 207. Ian Johnson, in a fine exhibition, took 7–44 in this innings. This left Australia 133 to win which they reached with the loss of Morris and McDonald. The pair again gave the side a good start with a partnership of 70, Morris batting in effortless style until caught at slip for 38 from the bowling of Norman Marshall. Harvey and Bill Watson piloted their side to the target. In the Tests to date, Arthur had totalled 259 from five innings, and he was also in the runs against the local Barbados side in a match before the fourth Test.

This game was played at Bridgetown, Barbados and produced some lively and exciting cricket before the Australians won by three wickets. Batting first, the Australians made 333. Morris batted at No 3 and made 33 in easy fashion before surprisingly being bowled. His second innings 78 was also easy on the eye and prompted Pat Landsberg to write: 'Morris is one of those astonishing batsmen who, on this tour, never looked as though he was going to get out, and indeed caused surprise when he did.' Weekes scored heavily in this match, making 100 out of 132 in two hours and finishing with 122, including 20 fours. He was particularly severe on Keith Miller.

At this stage of the tour, Morris was batting as well as he'd done for several seasons and it was unfortunate that he had to miss the fourth Test at Bridgetown. An attack of dysentery laid him low and he was far from well until the final Test back at Kingston was played about a month later. He had a couple of non-first-class games against the Windward and Leeward Islands but with indifferent success—scores of 3, 4 and 11 do not capture the eye.

The fourth Test, despite Morris's absence, was another high-scoring affair resulting in the inevitable draw. Batting first, the Australians made 668, Miller and Lindwall both making centuries, Ron Archer 98, Harvey 74 and Favell 72. West Indies replied with 510. Acting captain Atkinson demonstrated his skills in this innings. With the score at 6–146 and all the stars back in the pavilion, Atkinson and Clairmonte de Peiza, the wicket-keeper, were associated in an extraordinary seventh wicket stand of 347, batting for more than a full day. This is still a world record. Batting again, the Australians made 249, leaving the home side

408 runs to score for victory. At the end they were 6–234, Walcott again on view for 83. Atkinson added lustre to his batting by taking 5–56 in Australia's second innings and seven wickets for the match. There was some acrimony on the final day when Atkinson and Smith refused to run in an effort to avoid or postpone the taking of the new ball at 200 by Australia. Miller, never one to accept gamesmanship of this sort unchallenged, gave away four overthrows and bowled four wides in retaliation. This created a degree of alarm and anger among the spectators but was really a fair enough riposte to tactics not strictly in the spirit of the game.

The final Test at Kingston was marked again by heavy scoring by Australia and some fine batting by both sides. The home team dropped both Ramadhin and Valentine. The former retaliated by packing his bags forthwith and taking off to play in the Lancashire League. He returned to play for his country with success in following years. In stark contrast to the situation today, the West Indies suffered from a lack of both opening batsmen and opening bowlers. Failure to get a good start put pressure on those who followed and an amiable opening attack was money from home to the Australians despite the failure of Morris (lbw Tom Dewdney 7) and Favell, out hooking, for a duck. Harvey batted almost seven hours for 204, Archer, McDonald, Benaud and Miller all making centuries—five in an innings would take some beating. Benaud's 121 in 96 minutes was the fastest century in 52 years. The home side had already made 357, Walcott 155 and the other two 'Ws' 61 and 56. Weekes made his 56 in what was described as a 'ferocious' fashion until he was bowled around his legs, trying to sweep Benaud. Walcott's fourth century of the series occupied just under five hours with 23 fours. Bill Johnston damaged his knee in attempting to catch Walcott and had to be admitted to hospital. Walcott again hammered the bowling for 110, but apart from Sobers's 64 he played a lone hand in his team's total of 319. He was lucky in that nobody observed that he'd dislodged a bail at the conclusion of a hook shot but most would agree that his electrifying batting throughout the series had earned him a little luck. In totalling 827 for the series, Walcott trailed Bradman's 974 (England 1930), Hammond 905 (Australia 1928–29) and Harvey 834 (South Africa

1952–53). None of these three, however, had equalled Walcott's five centuries, made more remarkable in that in two matches he'd scored centuries in each innings.

It was reported that Arthur Morris had suffered from a couple of bad lbw decisions during the series and his total of 266 runs at 44.33 was well below the performances of Harvey, Miller and McDonald. Arthur accepted the doubtful decisions as being part and parcel of the game. Dissent was virtually unknown in his day and indeed until more than 20 years later. He took a philosophical view of the matter offsetting the bad decisions against possible 'let offs'. Surely this is the appropriate way to deal with a contentious side of cricket. Richie Benaud had a fine series with both bat and ball: 246 runs at 41 and 18 wickets at 27. Miller and Lindwall both captured wickets and Miller's double of 439 runs at 73.17 and 20 wickets at 32, made him only the third Australian to make over 400 runs and take 20 wickets in a series.

In the tour averages for first-class games, Morris was third with 577 runs at 52.45, behind Harvey and McDonald.

Ian Johnson had proved a charming and friendly captain, held in high regard by his colleagues and widely appreciated for his diplomatic and approachable attitude to press and public. Harmonious relationships among the three senior players extended throughout the side. The tour was to be Arthur Morris's swansong in first-class cricket. Matters of a personal nature had been concerning him for some time and were crucial in his deciding to quit the game. His first-class career, shortened by war, in effect lasted less than a decade and at the time of his retirement there was still a lot of good cricket left in him. But the seven years lost through war would probably have provided some of his finest batting judged by what he displayed, particularly in the early post-war years. As Sam Johnson said of his friend Oliver Goldsmith, Morris 'touched nothing that he did not adorn'. His cricket was played in the tradition of the great players from New South Wales. Starting with Trumper, the line goes through Macartney, Kippax, Jackson and McCabe and after Morris, continued in the play of Doug Walters. Of modern players the mantle will surely be inherited by Mark Waugh. If

Arthur did not quite exhibit Stan McCabe's lack of concern as to the progress of his own score, he was a worthy follower of Stan in the chivalrous and comradely attitude which marked his participation in a great game.

Morris

v

Bedser

a unique, lengthy but sporting confrontation

WHEN THE MERITS OF ARTHUR MORRIS are being discussed, much was made at the time (and even now) of his supposed vulnerability to Alec Bedser.

The two men were close friends during their cricketing careers and still are. They frequently meet, subject to distance, and sometimes stay under each other's roof when this is possible. Alec is about three years Morris's senior, so that his cricket probably suffered more from the lost war years than did Arthur's. Bedser was 28-years-old in 1946, Morris 25. Some word of his fame reached Australia following his success against the visiting Indians in the English summer of 1946. He had the remarkable haul of eleven wickets in each of the first two Tests he played. From this, no matter what the strength of the opposing batsmen (and in Lala Amarnath, Hazare and Merchant the side had its quota of good players), this was a performance of more than passing interest and concern to Australians.

What sort of a bowler was Bedser? If one answers that he was a worthy heir to Maurice Tate, it doesn't help greatly unless one was privileged to see both. I count myself among the lucky ones. When Tate came here in 1928, I was seven-years-old. Four years later he returned as a late, unwanted appendage to Douglas Jardine's 1932–33 side which wrought havoc and bitterness up and down the land. Tate played in the game against New South Wales and before lunch on the first day, dismissed Wendell Bill, Bradman and Kippax. After lunch he added McCabe to his haul. He was then 37-years-old. At the age of 11, the memory of his bowling that day is still clear—a big man who took a short run, delivered the ball with a high side-on action, at a pace not the equal of Larwood's (the yardstick for fast bowlers in those days) but lively enough, and seemed to hit the pitch pretty hard. From there it lifted sharply and veered away towards the slips. Tate also bowled the occasional inswinger but did not use it frequently. Alec Bedser, a rather bigger man than Tate, looked immensely powerful, a slightly larger edition of Graham McKenzie. Tate had sloping shoulders, Bedser's are square. Tate had cricket's biggest feet, Bedser boasted an enormous pair of hands.

Bedser had a splendid side-on action not unlike Tate's—arm pointing heavenwards, head looking at the batsman over his left shoulder. He measured off a run of 13 paces and his approach was perhaps a little more laboured than Tate's. Both bowled a brisk medium-fast. Bedser's stock ball was the inswinger, which for Morris, went away late towards slips. His outswinger was a rarity. Instead, quite by accident when bowling to Sid Barnes in 1946–47, one delivery which as usual had ducked in late from Barnes's offside, hit the pitch and veered back to graze his off stump. Barnes was dumbfounded. Ever the pragmatist and never diffident on or off the cricket field, Barnes called up the pitch to Bedser: 'Eh, what the hell's going on?'

This was the birth of the leg cutter, a delivery which, if it pitches on the right spot, is virtually unplayable. A delighted Bedser used it in Adelaide to bowl Bradman who still maintains that this particular delivery was the best he'd ever received. Naturally it became a significant weapon in Bedser's arsenal, never to be over-used but unleashed as a surprise and unsettling variation on his main theme.

This new delivery, indistinguishable from the hand, obviously added to Arthur Morris's problem with Bedser. It added a new factor in the tally of ways he could get out. With the standard outswinger, there was always the chance that he'd get an edge to the wicket-keeper, or slip—particularly when he hadn't gone across and back far enough to avoid being left in no-man's land and forced into the half-cock prod. The leg-cutter could find Morris leg before or, very occasionally, bowled behind his legs if he was too far across.

Alec Bedser, in his book *Cricket Choice*, generously credits Morris with immaculate judgment playing back or driving, and considered his batting 'flawless' in 1946–47. Later Alec bowled a fuller length to take advantage of movement in the air and, armed with the leg cutter, tried to get Morris to commit himself to his stroke before the direction of swing was apparent. With an element of uncertainty in Morris's mind, says Bedser, he tended to 'shuffle' sideways to the off leaving himself open to a catch at leg slip if he'd had to adjust quickly for the cutter, or at worst, see his leg stump in disarray.

In a recent letter Alec Bedser makes the point again that, as an opening bowler, it was not surprising that he should have his fair share of success with Morris. He adds that he also trapped the other great left-hander, Neil Harvey, frequently—indeed in the twenty Test innings when the two were opposed, Bedser had Harvey twelve times, or in 60% of the encounters, compared with Morris's eighteen Test dismissals from 37 confrontations. Bradman was not entirely impervious to Bedser's wiles and stated that he had found Bedser a more difficult bowler than Tate. We have it from Jack Fingleton that Maurice was a little hurt at Bradman's assessment. Bradman played against Tate in 1928–29 and 1930, both heavy-scoring series, when Maurice was probably past his best, while Bradman was at his extraordinary peak. On the other hand, the Don was in his late thirties when he found Bedser troublesome, whereas the bowler had reached *his* peak.

Ian Johnson was a member of Bradman's all-conquering 1948 side. He recalls batting with Arthur in the Old Trafford Test. He was called on to open Australia's second innings in place of Barnes who'd been hit hard in the ribs, while fielding at short leg, by Dick Pollard—a blow Sid modestly declared 'would have killed any ordinary man'. Ian writes:

> 'There had been a little rain and the pitch was just a bit responsive. Arthur took strike to Alec Bedser who moved the ball both ways, in the air and off the pitch. He hit every

159

ball of that first over in the middle. At over's end, he came down the pitch and said: 'It's doing a bit. We'd better stick around or Alec could run through us.' I replied: 'OK but if we have to do that, you keep Alec. I'd have no hope against him the way he's bowling'. And I meant it! Then for best part of an hour we did stay there and, in all that time, I did not receive one ball from Alec Bedser. Arthur took them all and it allowed me to watch from the bowler's end, the most fascinating exhibition I have ever seen. Bedser bowled superbly yet Arthur middled every ball in the finest display of defensive batting you could imagine. Here were two champions at their peak and although Alec was not disgraced, Arthur won the day.'

Ian Johnson adds that Morris frequently protected other batsmen but invariably did it in a most unobtrusive way.

Bedser and Morris never failed to remind each other, in a friendly fashion, of their 'successes'. Frank Tyson writes that Bedser still reminds Arthur, even when they meet now, of his eighteen dismissals in the seven years of Anglo-Australian Test cricket they enjoyed. Arthur makes the perfect reply that, while Bedser was getting him out, he notched eight of his twelve Test centuries against Bedser and his colleagues.*

During the 1950–51 Test series when Arthur fell five times to Bedser in the Tests and twice in other games, there was much media talk about his 'Bedser hoodoo'. Arthur was a little sensitive about this, and he was scoring prolifically in games other than the Tests. Consequently, his 206 in the fourth Test at Adelaide was a great confidence-booster and he went on to get 50 in the first innings of the final Test, only to fall victim to 'The Lion of Surrey' in their last encounter of the season.

Arthur Morris's regard for Bedser, both as bowler and friend, is very high. He considers that Bedser took a little time to settle into his

---

* These eight centuries against England were compiled in 43 innings. This record fell in 1982 when Greg Chappell notched his ninth century against England, but in his 61st innings.

Newcastle Boys High School 1st XI, 1934. Morris, aged 12, seated at right front.

Hutton cuts past Arthur at Lord's, 1953.

Two of a kind. Tate and Bedser in the delivery stride.

Bradman and Morris resume after lunch on the last day at Leeds, 1948. The pair added 301, and were decisive in an historic victory.

The hook shot as played by Morris, 1946. Arthur thinks the bowler was England, lefthander, Bill Voce.

Opening with Ken Archer SCG. Evans is the 'keeper.

Ian Johnson (Victoria) appeals enthusiastically (but unsuccessfully) for lbw against Morris at a Melbourne Shield Match. From Arthur's position the appeal appears optimistic.

Arthur with former England captain Peter May, at a State
Bank reception 1988.

Lindsay Hassett, Arthur, Geoff Noblet, Freddie Brown—State
Bank reception, 1988.

**Through mid-wicket—CG Macartney considered this stroke to
be one of the 'hallmarks of batsmanship'.**

First post-war Australian XI, Brisbane, 1946.

The St George 1940/41 first XI. This star studded side could have, at a pinch, represented Australia.

bowling groove and was at his best in about the third over of a bowling spell. His stamina was exceptional and his workload heavy. The actual overs bowled in his four Ashes series against Australia were:

Australia 1946–47 _ **242 overs (eight ball)**
England 1948 _____ **274 overs (six ball)**
Australia 1950–51 _ **195 overs (eight ball)**
England 1953 _____ **265 overs (six ball)**

For purposes of workload comparisons, the following recent figures are interesting:

6 Tests England 1989 _____ **Alderman 269 overs (six ball)**
_____ **Lawson 277 overs (six ball)**
4 Tests Australia 1990 _____ **Hughes 142 overs (six ball)**
_____ **Reid 180 overs (six ball)**

Bedser's workloads are clearly heavier.

On the two Australian tours of 1946–47 and 1950–51, the overs comprised eight balls, in England six. Morris found him very effective even when the ball was old.

Bill O'Reilly always maintained that, in his duels with Bradman, he 'came out square'. He would not have bowled to Bradman nearly as many times as Bedser bowled to Morris, and of course never in Test cricket. Arthur Morris, if one wants to get down to figures, came out more than square. Phil Derriman, in his book *The Top 100 and the First XI*, calculates that in Morris's thirty-seven Test innings when Bedser was playing, he averaged 57.42 while his opening partners lumped together averaged 35.57. A similar comparison for all forty-six first-class innings shows Morris with an average of 61, his opening partners 46.

Ray Robinson's book *On Top Down Under*, gives brief biographies of Australian Test captains since early days. Morris, despite his comparatively few outings as Australian captain, gets a fairly long and highly complimentary coverage. Commenting on Arthur's 'shuffle', Robinson thinks that it led him to play at deliveries he might well have disregarded, with the occasional slip catch resulting. He recalls that, in a Launceston match in early 1951 between MCC and a Combined Eleven, Bedser got Morris cheaply in both innings. At the game's conclusion, Bedser gave Arthur a book on *Better Cricket* written jointly by Lindsay Hassett and Ian Johnson. Bedser carefully marked passages in the batting section for Arthur's edification. A week or two later Arthur broke a run of outs with his long innings of 206 in the Test match in Adelaide. On the evening of the second day of the match, he returned the book to Bedser with the section on bowling carefully marked. Bedser's figures for the innings 26–4–74–3 were good—but his victims did not include Arthur Morris.

The contests between the two fascinated the pundits and the public for four Test series. One finds it hard to discover a parallel among opening batsmen when pitted against opening bowlers. Herbie Collins fell to Maurice Tate six times in ten encounters in 1924–25, and Mailey accounted for Sutcliffe five times out of nine in the same series. But there appears to be no other instance where an opening batsman has confronted an opening bowler nearly as many times as Morris faced Bedser between 1946 and 1954.*

Over the years, Morris had observed that if there were any easy runs to be gained from Bedser, it would be advisable to gather them early in his spell. By the third over Alec was in the groove, dropping the ball just short of driveable length but far enough up to make the back stroke a matter of quick decision and quicker action. The leg cutter, Bedser's contribution to the bowler's art, was always prominent in Arthur's mind—would it be the next ball, or the next, or when? While the cutter, properly pitched to the right hander, a fast leg break in fact, is a nightmare delivery, threatening the bat's edge for the slip catch or collecting the off stump, it had hazards of a different kind for Morris. It could find him lbw, or bowl him behind his leg as he played for the outswinger. These thoughts were never far from his mind as he faced the great bowler. There haven't been many bowlers of this type. Since Bedser, Alderman would probably be the best. He varied his outswinger (to the right hander) with a beautifully concealed delivery that

---

* Other occasions which come to mind in England vs Australia Tests are: *Hobbs v Gregory* 1920–21—1928–29; *Boycott v McKenzie* 1964—1970–71; *Boycott v Lillee* 1970–71—1981; *McDonald v Trueman* 1953—1961

came straight on and lbw's to Alderman were frequent—19 out of 41 Test wickets in 1989. Medium pacers have to be very good to be any good. Barnes, Tate, Bedser and Alderman are the four who come to mind.

Both men would agree that the overall outcome could fairly be called 'all square'. It may be appropriate to conclude this chapter by noting that Arthur Morris bowled Alec Bedser in the farcical Old Trafford Test of 1953. His remark: 'I never knew it was so easy.'

Of Style

and

Other Things

'All styles are good except the tiresome sort'—Voltaire

JOHN PARKER, AN ENGLISH WRITER, who gave us a couple
of novelettes on village cricket in his native land, also compiled an
interesting book entitled *Cricket, Styles and Stylists.* In it he starts by
defining style when applied to cricketers and then goes back to the days
of W G Grace and C B Fry. Predictably names like Ranji, Maclaren,
Woolley, Trumper, Macartney, McCabe and Hammond figure promi-
nently among batsmen. Colin Blythe, Rhodes, Lindwall, Tate, Barnes,
McDonald, Bedser and O'Reilly are some of the bowlers. Among left-
handers, Parker considers Arthur Morris the most 'elegant' to grace the
scene since Woolley. As the book was written in 1979, the period produced some pretty good ones—Leyland, Paynter, Harvey, Sobers, John
Edrich and Bill Lawry are a few.

　　An interesting aside to Parker's book is his reporting that Richie
Benaud in his World Eleven discovered, somewhat to his surprise, that
all the batsmen he'd picked were back-foot players. Morris was predominantly a back-foot player. So were Bradman, McCabe, Ponsford,
Harvey and Greg Chappell. All hated to be forced into a forward stroke
except to drive. It was Arthur Morris's good fortune to cut his first-class
cricket teeth under the guidance of Stan McCabe. McCabe could drive
handsomely on both sides of the wicket and when he did, his left foot

was so close to the ball that he could have trodden on it. Later, Morris batted at some length and on numerous occasions with Bradman, the greatest player of all. Don was rarely forced on to his front foot except when he drove. It is interesting to note that, in his last Test innings, Eric Hollies lured him forward in defence and bowled him second ball, an event of almost earthshaking significance.

Statistics, like it or not, can't be refuted out of hand. They tell only part of a man's cricket, but it's an important part. Statistically, Morris's cricket peaked in the years 1946–1950 and there-after there was a perceptible decline, even though there were periods after 1950 when he scored prolifically again. However at no time did he forsake the style which was the hallmark of his batsmanship. He never offended the eye and, even when out of touch, the fundamental class of his play was clearly apparent.

Ian Johnson thought he peaked in 1948 and in his book *Cricket at the Crossroads*, wrote that he was the equal of any left-hander of any time. Johnson believed that if Morris, Bradman and Hassett had been playing, Jim Laker's harvest of wickets in 1956 would have been far fewer. One does not need to be an Einstein to conclude that, in the 1956 team, only Neil Harvey could be classed with the three mentioned and the outcome of the series would probably have been different. Ian Johnson says he never found a satisfactory solution to his difficulties in bowling to Arthur and he attributes this to the slight touch of unortho-doxy in his batting. For example when driving, Arthur's foot was not as close to his bat as McCabe's had been, or as the text book lays down. This should have left a gap which could be exploited. Denis Compton was the same and Johnson had problems with him too.

In a recent letter, Ian rated Morris with Len Hutton as the finest opening batsmen since World War II. Since his earlier book, he has varied his opinion only to place Sobers equal with Morris among left-handers. 'He (Morris) always had so much time to play his shots and was never hurried. He watched the ball more carefully than most and invariably seemed to play late. Like Stan McCabe, he caressed the ball rather than hit it yet, such was his timing, that is sped on its way with incredible speed.' Johnson remembered bowling to McCabe in 1938.

One particular delivery was played, so it seemed, defensively by Stan and Ian Johnson turned to walk back to his bowling mark expecting the ball to be returned by the cover fieldsman. 'To my great surprise the latter was picking it up as it rebounded from the fence.'

At the personal level, Ian Johnson found Arthur Morris more like Stan McCabe than any other person he met. 'Like Stan, he was quiet, reserved yet possessed strong determination. He had the same friendly outlook on life and rarely, if ever, offered criticism even of people of whom, you knew, he disapproved.' It seems Arthur sought and found the good which, we believe, is present is everybody, but this endearing trait did not affect the determination with which he would fight for a cause in which he believed.

Ian Johnson has much more to say about Morris, the man. The two have been friends since the late forties. Ian says that, in his day as skipper of the New South Wales State side, Arthur showed obvious embarrassment at times at the frequency with which his fast bowlers let fly with bouncers. With Lindwall, Miller and Alan Walker, the NSW side had a virtual monopoly of fast men and all three were disinclined to restrict their bouncers to the imprecise level which the rules then allowed. Johnson says that Arthur would not interfere, despite his embarrassment, feeling that it was the umpire's job to interpret the rule. There was an exception however. Morris would tactfully intervene when he felt that tail-end players were being assaulted.

It seems that Morris was an ideal team man, particularly on tour when there are inevitably difficulties between some members at times. With his quiet, equable personality, he was invaluable in smoothing out this sort of niggling dispute. He was a worthy ambassador for his country—polite and urbane in manner, articulate and intelligent enough to converse easily on a variety of topics apart from cricket, he made an excellent impression on his hosts and this, of course, was good for Australia. This was particularly the case when, as third selector in the West Indies, the pair with vice-captain Miller did much to remove the somewhat sour taste left by the MCC team which had toured the previous year.

Johnson concluded his letter: 'For something like ten years in a row after the war, New South Wales played Victoria in Melbourne over Christmas. On all but one of these occasions, Arthur and Ray Lindwall came to our home for Christmas dinner. Yet this friendship never prevented Arthur from handing it out to me the day before or the day after Christmas, nor did it stop Ray Lindwall from dishing out more than a fair share of bumpers at me.'

Bill O'Reilly, of course, probably knew Arthur better than did any other cricketer. Bill virtually 'discovered' him and quickly concluded that the mixture of slow left-hand off breaks that he was sending down in the lower grades of the St George Club was only a minor adjunct to the spectacular, latent talent he showed so clearly when he handled a bat. O'Reilly, never one to dawdle when his mind was made up, quickly brought this bowling nonsense to a sudden stop. Before he knew what had happened, Arthur was elevated in the batting order, struck off the bowling agenda and, to his shock and dismay one Saturday, instructed by the 'Tiger' to pad up and open the St George innings.

Arthur Morris's record at the St George Club is a notable one. A great admirer, Warren Saunders, St George and New South Wales player of the fifties and sixties, idolised Arthur Morris whom he first saw as a teenager. He wrote recently that Arthur was a 'magnificent example to the young players in the Club, a superb cricketer whose conduct on and off the field as always exemplary.'

Warren traced Arthur's progress at St George from 1936–37 until he quit to join Paddington at the conclusion of the 1951–52 season. Playing in the A W Green Shield (under 16) team in 1936–37, he won both batting and bowling averages, and the following season progressed to the First XI for the final few games. Thereafter he was a permanent member of the First XI. In 1938–39 he topped the Poidevin–Gray Shield batting averages with 476 runs at an average of 119.

The Club's annual report for 1938–39 noted:

> A Morris totalled 433 runs at an average of 33.3 and played many excellent innings. Like the majority of left-handers, he is strong on the leg side. His 115 against University was

a delightful innings and earned him a place in the New South Wales 2nd Eleven which played Victoria in Melbourne. Being a first-class slip fieldsman and a good left-hand slow bowler, this player is the most promising all-rounder St George has discovered for many years.

In 1940–41 Arthur scored 890 runs for the club, a record which stood until Brad McNamara and Geoff Milliken broke it in 1990–91.

Warren Saunders continues: 'Arthur was a member of the St George team which won four 1st grade premierships. In first grade he scored 4552 and was dismissed exactly 100 times and so his average was 45.52. His highest score was 201 n.o. and he made 13 centuries. Also he holds the Green shield record when in 1937–38 he took an amazing 55 wickets at an average of 5.23.'

While on the subject of Arthur's District Club career, which certainly was an important element in grooming him for representative honours, it is interesting to note Len Hutton's views on our cricket at the district level. Hutton expressed the opinion to Arthur that Australia's superiority when compared with England was due in large measure to the District competitions, particularly in capital and provincial cities. This has no parallel in England where there would surely be many promising players at club or even 'Village Green' level, who never get the chance to display their wares in the County system. Hutton added a cautionary note, namely that this Australian advantage may be in the process of erosion because of the frequency with which good players are required for representative fixtures, to the detriment of their District clubs.

Bill O'Reilly always considered that there have been few better openers than Arthur Morris. In his 'best ever' Australian side, listed in Phil Derriman's book, *The Top 100 and First Eleven*, he has Morris down to open with Ponsford. Bill always considered Ponsford a more difficult problem to bowl to than Bradman. Bill said Don gave the bowler a chance, Ponsford exhibited no such kindness.

O'Reilly thought that during the period when Alec Bedser was troubling Arthur, the latter's difficulty stemmed from the habit he'd developed of 'playing Bedser on the run' and getting frequent edges. On the whole though, Bill agreed that the pair broke even. For one who regarded Stan McCabe as without peer among batsmen, he paid Arthur a great compliment by classing him with Stan as the two finest hookers he saw.

Bill had been close to Arthur ever since the two met in the thirties. They played tennis together regularly as well as cricket and Bill had a warm regard for one whom he could justly claim to have put on the right track as a cricketer. It's possible, but not likely, that Arthur would have scaled the heights as a bowler. That he did as a batsman is largely due to W J O'Reilly. Like the Pope when he speaks 'Ex Cathedra', Bill had claims to infallibility when he judged cricketers.

Lindsay Hassett, close friend of Stan McCabe and Bill O'Reilly, and almost as good a player as Stan in his carefree pre-war days, had quite a lot to say about Arthur Morris. Typically, Hassett started by declaring that no matter how hard he strained his memory, he couldn't recall one really nasty cricketer he played with or against in his twenty years of first-class cricket. He was, of course, a widely loved man and it would be hard to find anyone to speak unkindly of him—he reaped as he sowed. Lindsay went on: 'I would have to name Arthur Morris as one of the most pleasant (cricketers) of them all. On top of that, he must be classed among the very best opening batsmen of my time.' Hassett played with or against such openers as Woodfull, Ponsford, Brown, Barnes and Fingleton of Australians and Hutton, Washbrook, C J Barnett and McGlew of opponents. 'No batsman ever presented more of the full face of the bat either in defence or in "front of the wicket" scoring strokes.' Lindsay himself was as near perfect technically as any batsman, so he would set a high standard.

Hassett thought Arthur was a fine team man who was loyal to his mates and completely unassuming concerning his own ability. 'I always enjoyed playing with him rather than against him', said Lindsay, 'but win or lose, he never harmed the "Spirit of Cricket" passed on to us by those who'd gone before.'

Lindsay Hassett recalled a match between New South Wales and Victoria at the Sydney Cricket Ground. He and Arthur were the captains and the curator had turned on the greenest and fastest wicket Lindsay had ever encountered. He thought the fact that New South Wales had a bowling attack comprising Lindwall, Miller, Alan Walker and Alan Davidson, a fairly lively quartet, may have influenced the curator to some degree.

'Bumpers flew at a furious pace but there was not the slightest evidence of "sledging" ', he went on. 'At one stage I halted Keith Miller's approach to the bowling crease and said to Herb Elphinstone, the umpire: "What about this law against intimidation?" There was no positive response from Herb but the interruption only added fuel to Miller's fire. Ian Johnson, my partner, faced the last three balls of the over and all of them whistled past his ears.'

It was customary in those long lost days for the home skipper to invite the opposition over to the home dressing-room for a drink at the conclusion of a game. Lindsay thought that an unusually long time had elapsed without an invitation, so he sent a note over to Arthur Morris which put the question: 'Aren't you going to turn on a drink?' Arthur Morris replied by return mail, so to speak: 'Yes—by all means—bring them in, bruises and all.' Lindsay kept Arthur's note and he remembered that the next hour or so was 'spent in the usual atmosphere of good fellowship.' One may hope that this type of camaraderie still exists, but I've heard nothing to suggest it does. Lindsay Hassett concluded that 'Morris had brilliance and modesty in the most generous proportions, and I'm sure that the cricket field has never been graced by a finer gentleman.' More about Hassett later.

Sam Loxton had a fairly restricted playing acquaintance with Morris but regarded him as 'one of the greats of the game, as a player and a person.' Sam says he's made up for the comparative restrictions on their playing days in common by hammering Arthur's ear to good effect in their frequent post–cricket encounters.

Bill Johnston and Arthur Morris are 'twins' in two senses. They were born within four weeks of each other and both shared a fairly uncommon physical characteristic in that they did everything left-handed. Bill, tongue in cheek, harks back to his batting average of 102 on the 1953 tour of England, whimsically contrived by skipper Lindsay

Hassett. Lindsay's main problem at the end of the tour was to ensure that Bill got out once in order to have an average at all. Arthur recalls his own bowling figures of 5 wickets for 10 against Scotland and both men consider that they were the only genuine left-handed all-rounders Australia had produced at that time—though Alan Davidson's appearance soon after would have changed that. A quick assessment of this physical attribute in modern times brings to mind Allan Border of Australia, Gary Sobers of the West Indies and, further back, Frank Woolley of England. But in the days of Johnston and Morris, Neil Harvey and Slasher Mackay, both bowled right-handed and batted left-handed.

Johnston confirms the thoughts of others with regard to Arthur's personality and ease in accumulating friends on and off the cricket field. He credits him with an acute cricket brain, demonstrated by his showing when skippering sides on tour when Hassett was standing down. Further, he joins with his Victorian team mate, Ian Johnson, in bracketing Arthur with Hutton as the two best openers he saw. 'He was never afraid to commit himself to a full-blooded shot if the ball warranted it, even if it was the first delivery he received.' Johnston frequently opened the bowling for Victoria against New South Wales when Morris and Barnes were the openers. He thought Arthur the more dangerous of the two and he usually 'showed the way'. This is no disparagement of Barnes, who in big games usually subdued his natural instincts in what he saw as his team's interests. There have been few more punishing players off the back foot than Sid Barnes. However he was not a great driver of the ball, which must place him below the 'complete' players like McCabe, Bradman and Morris.

Bill Brown was one of the most correct and elegant players of his time. An opening batsman, he looked the complete player—bat perpendicular, head over the ball, straight back-lift and so on. His leg glance was as famous as Kippax's late cut or McCabe's hook. Nobody has glanced with more ease and delicacy than Bill Brown. His Test average from 1592 runs at 46.82 sits well with 13,838 first-class runs at 51.44. He relished English wickets—in 1934 he scored 1308 runs at 38, in 1938 he made 1854 runs at 58 and, with Bradman's 1948 team, he had

1448 runs, again at 58. It is a striking indication of the strength of the 1948 tourists that Barnes was preferred to Brown as an opener and that in the last two Tests, Neil Harvey replaced him in the No 6 batting spot. Illness limited his international cricket in Australia.

As was noted earlier, Bill Brown took little time to conclude that, in Arthur Morris, Australia had a potential champion. On the second occasion that he saw him, Arthur made two centuries in the same match against Queensland (the first time this had been performed by a player in his initial first-class game). Bill Brown was the Queensland skipper. An extensive examination of Arthur's batting in that match confirmed Bill's opinion that 'he had every shot in the book and, what's more, he could play them with ease'. Morris's 290 at Bristol against Gloucester in 1948, on a turning wicket, was another remarkable feat. Tom Goddard, the County's renowned off spinner, was in line for Test selection at the time but his figures when Morris had finished with him put paid to this possibility. Bill Brown, who should know, points out that when comparing players, the fact that some were called upon to open the innings whenever they batted should be taken into account. It was Morris's fate, as well as Brown's, to experience this. There are factors in opening that are not present in the lower batting positions.

Frank Tyson ranks with Jeff Thomson and Harold Larwood in terms of speed. It would be hard to separate them, and in Australia in 1954–55, Tyson bowled as fast or faster than anyone in the game's history. He never again reached the level of that Australian season. Watching him bowl, one could not help but feel apprehensive regarding the batsman's uncertain hold on life as the thunderbolts whistled through, usually at chest height or above. A genial and gregarious man off the field, Tyson has this to say about Arthur Morris: 'Arthur Morris is one of cricket's patricians. As a person and a player, he is endowed with a genteel equanimity, without seeming aloof or less than cordial and friendly. He regarded cricket as a sporting experience in which knowledge and enjoyment are shared. He was never averse to discussing the game even with his opponents—a characteristic which made him a surprising number of friends.'

Tyson says Arthur enjoyed a warm friendship with Freddie Brown, who died in July of 1991. As we have noted, Freddie got pleasure from watching Morris's first confrontation with Tyson at Northampton in 1953. On that occasion, Morris experienced something of what England players had endured from 1946 on when facing Lindwall and Miller. Tyson found Arthur a consistent punisher of the loose ball but rock solid in defence and a quick-footed player of slow bowling. It seems like a perfect combination for an opener.

Ray Robinson was probably the most eloquent of Australian cricket writers. In some ways, notably the penning of a particularly apt or memorable phrase or adjective, he was comparable with Neville Cardus. His knowledge of cricket was greater than Cardus's but the quality of Neville's prose takes some beating. In Robinson's book, *Green Sprigs*, written in 1954, he pointed out that there are certain difficulties inherent in the scoring of two centuries in one's initial first-class match. A standard is set which one is expected to live up to. Contrary to Morris, Len Hutton with whom Arthur is generally linked as the finest openers of their time, was run out for 0 in his first game for Yorkshire at the tender age of 17. Maurice Leyland, a cheery soul, comforted him— 'Never mind Leonard—tha's started at the bottom.' Arthur kept his head after his early success. The long war years gave him ample time in which to cool off.

Robinson recorded that Bradman reproved Morris for having a beer after a day's play in 1948. 'That won't bring you many runs,' said the Don. The words may have been spoken in jest but they are consistent with Bradman's attitude in those days—an attitude, it has to be said, that may have lost him more friends than it gained.

Interestingly, Ray Robinson said that Neil Harvey, at his best, still considered Morris his superior as a batsman. This is a generous appraisal, for Harvey was a glorious player and some of his innings rank with the best every played. In Derriman's book referred to earlier, seven good judges of cricketers were asked to pick their 'best Australian XI ever'. Of the seven, four chose Morris to open the batting: Alan McGilvray, Hunter Hendry, Phil Ridings and Cliff Winning. Of batsmen, only Bradman (7), Trumper (6) and Miller (5) got more votes than Arthur. As Miller was an all-rounder, most selectors picked him primarily as such. This leaves only Bradman and Trumper ahead of Morris. Most people would rate those two as our greatest batsmen so that Arthur comes in third in a very distinguished field. It's interesting that only three players gained selection in all seven judges' teams—Bradman, O'Reilly and Don Tallon.

The United Kingdom *Cricketer*, a journal of some prestige, points out in its May 1947 issue, that only Archie Jackson was younger than Arthur in making two centuries in a first-class game. Jackson was 18 years 4 months, Morris 18 years 11 months. Arthur Morris would be proud to be bracketed with Jackson, a frail batting genius whose life was cut short by tuberculosis when he was 22. Jackson was, as Cardus would say, 'in the line of Trumper,' his batting all elegance and concealed power. We who saw Jackson and McCabe bat are lucky, those who saw Trumper and Jackson luckier still. Some said that he'd have been as heavy a scorer as Bradman but this is doubtful. It's doubtful whether anyone will match Bradman in sheer ability to amass runs. The runs Jackson would have scored would have been fewer but they'd have had more style. The batsmen with that special style seem to come from New South Wales—Trumper, Macartney, Kippax, Jackson, McCabe and Morris. Neil Harvey, a Victorian, would fit comfortably into this great company—the exception that proves the rule. Of present day players Mark Waugh, as previously noted, may join this select band.

The cricketers' version of Holy Writ, *Wisden's Almanack*, in its 1949 issue, could scarcely avoid naming Morris as one of its five 'Cricketers of the Year' (ie in 1948). They were all Australians that year—the others Lindwall, Hassett, Bill Johnston and Tallon. This honour is only bestowed once to any cricketer and the honour is widely sought after and greatly treasured. Wisden said of Morris that his feats in England in 1948 provided 'the final qualification which led to his assessment as one of the world's best left-hand batsmen.' Nobody would disagree with this assessment except to say that Morris was *the* best—in 1948 there was no left-hander in the same class playing the game. All the possible challengers had gone and Neil Harvey had only just arrived.

Wisden continued that Morris had more fluency than Bardsley and was 'imposing to opponents and impressive to spectators due to his air of complete composure at the wicket.' It adds that his placements lost little by comparison with Bradman.

Tom Graveney, a batsman of the top flight in his native land but not so successful in Australia, probably because of his preference for playing off the front foot, was playing for Gloucester in the match which Morris adorned with his 290. Graveney described the display as 'breathtaking'. He considered Goddard a 'devastating' bowler, particularly on his home wicket, but he was completely collared this day.

Arthur was Richie Benaud's first captain at first-class level. Richie's father, Lou, a leg spinner of note at District Club level, introduced Arthur to his son while the latter was still at school. Arthur was freshly demobilised and back in the State side. Richie remembers saying nervously, 'How are you Mr Morris,' the type of greeting which was usual at that time. Arthur replied, 'Don't call me Mr Morris! My name is Arthur.'

When Richie received his first New South Wales cap in 1948 with Morris captain, the match was played on a 'green top' against Queensland and Lindwall, Miller and Walker carried too many guns for the Queenslanders. Richie didn't get a bowl. He recalls Morris's hurricane second innings century in 82 minutes referred to elsewhere. Richie says it was a 'marvellous' century on a pitch that had defied the efforts of batsmen of both sides until Morris took charge. Later Arthur apologised to Benaud for not having given him a bowl—he hadn't been needed with the fast bowlers dominant.

Fifteen years later, Richie skippered a Commonwealth side to tour South Africa, Rhodesia and India. Ron Roberts, the cricket writer, had organised the tour and the side included England captain, Ted Dexter, and New Zealand captain, John Reid. It was the first occasion on which three current Test captains had played together in a first-class game. Arthur Morris, then aged 42, and absent from first-class cricket for eight years, damaged a hamstring early in the piece but blossomed later against India in Bombay. In the course of Morris's dazzling 70, Norman O'Neill called four of the team on to the balcony to see Morris in action. 'Don't miss a ball of this,' said O'Neill, 'this bloke was one of the greatest and he played with my club.' This exhortation reminds one of Bradman's call to his team mates when Stan McCabe was demolishing England's bowlers at Trent Bridge in 1938.

Richie continues that since 1948, he rates Morris and Neil Harvey as having the most 'outstanding' footwork of the players he's seen. They were equally good against speed or spin and he puts them ahead even of such classy performers as Everton Weekes and Gary Sobers. As player and commentator, Benaud has seen a few batsmen since 1948. He considers Morris 'a good hooker and puller, fearless against the fastest bowlers. Morris's timing gave the impression of effortless ease in all his strokes. He caressed rather than bludgeoned the ball when driving.' Richie endorses the opinions of all Morris's colleagues and contemporaries that he combined cricketing skill with personal qualities of loyalty and modesty in his character. In Miller, Lindwall and Morris, he had the 'wisest, hardest, toughest, most sympathetic, generous and helpful mentors one could ask for.'

With the aid of glasses, pepper and salt shakers, Arthur would demonstrate over a beer or two where he thought Richie might have gone wrong, either with his batting or bowling during the day. One might say that Richie Benaud is an unshakeable admirer of Arthur Morris, both as a cricketer and a man, a feeling shared, it seems, by all with whom Arthur played. Benaud speaks highly of Arthur's character: 'completely honest, a great friend, he's never let anyone down and is completely unassuming, just as he was on the cricket field.'

Ian Craig's experience of playing with Arthur is necessarily brief because of the age difference between the two. However he toured England with Morris in Hassett's 1953 team and admired him as a colleague and batsman. He served on the SCG Trust with Arthur for a number of years when Morris and Pat Hills were heavily involved in upgrading the old ground. Craig remembers Arthur warning Jim Burke and Richie Benaud against mixing marriage with a cricketing career—the two had just announced their engagements. But Arthur fell for Val Hudson in England in 1953 and later married her.

Craig considered that Arthur was 'a bit of a worrier' at the start of a match, an opinion which Morris considers 'very perspicacious.' He agrees that he was always nervous for twenty-four hours before an important match. 'I needed a few beers the night before in order to sleep and not play my innings throughout the night.' He is sure that even if uncomfortable, it was a good thing to have the adrenalin pumping because 'it makes you sharper. Without the nervous jitters,' Arthur says, 'I rarely performed well. When I walked to the wicket,' he continues, 'I didn't think of the runs I would score but rather whether I'd survive.' After he got bat on ball, his confidence returned and the jitters vanished. Most participants in competitive sport, at most levels, would experience something similar. For example, Arthur recalls Bill Brown and Neil Harvey recently confiding to each other that from time to time they'd dream that it is their turn to bat and they can't find their bats! Most of us can relate in some way to this sort of frustrating dream and to the relief experienced when the alarm clock wakes us.

Arthur was instrumental in having Ian's name brought forward as a replacement on the Cricket Ground Trust when Stan McCabe died in 1968. The matter was first raised at Stan's funeral service.

The two play tennis together regularly, still with Arthur dictating play, his younger opponents doing most of the running. Morris quite often plays six sets of tennis which is no mean feat at three score years and ten plus.

Ian differs from Morris in his opinion of off spinners. Arthur thought Laker the best he faced while he found Hugh Tayfield slightly mechanical; Ian Craig, who batted against both quite a few times, thinks the opposite. It should be added that Arthur, with his quick-footedness, found most spinners 'money from home' despite the fact that the off spinner came from Morris's leg or blind side. 'One man's meat is another man's poison' appears appropriate here. Both Tayfield and Laker were fine exponents of off spin, certainly the best of their time.

On the matter of finger spinners, either left or right hand, Morris firmly believed in attack. 'On good wickets,' he says, 'they have little spin and rely on accuracy. To push forward and allow them to dictate is to court disaster. They can bring fieldsmen in close to wait for the "bat pad" catch, so it's essential to go after them and not allow them to settle into an awkward length. Whenever I read of an off spinner bowling badly, I know that the batsmen have prevented him from bowling his own line and direction. It's not so much that the bowler has bowled badly but rather that the batsmen have called his bluff.' Of course, if the wicket is taking spin, the finger spinner will come into his own.

Arthur Morris's personality, relaxed and modest, would probably have felt little disappointment at not being a long serving Australian captain, thinks Ian Craig. As vice-captain, he was a captain's delight— reliable, capable, unflappable, well liked and quite unlikely to do anything without weighing the issues involved.

To round off this chapter, who better to turn to than John Arlott, beloved commentator and writer, and a wine buff of note? In 1948 when the post-war Bradman was seemingly well on his way to another century at Lord's (he was out at 89 to a sinfully acrobatic slip catch by Bill Edrich), he at one stage held up play while several players gathered around to assist Bradman remove something from his eye. Arlott commented in his West Country drawl, 'Now Bradman has something in his eye. The players are all gathered around him to help in removing it. Many of us over here think Bradman should be *made* to bat with something in his eye.'

Of Arthur Morris, Arlott wrote in *Wisden's Cricket Monthly* in November 1983: 'Morris was a left-hander of many strokes, but one who never thought cricket was more important than life. He suffered some ill luck and at least one major tragedy, but he bore all problems bravely. He is one of the few great cricketers about whom one's first reaction is to admire him as a human being.' Arlott goes on to recall Morris's sacrifice of his own wicket at 99 against South Africa in 1952–53, so that his younger partner would not be run out. Arlott goes on to an analysis of Morris's batting: 'He commanded all the strokes, played them freely off front or back foot, hooking, driving and cutting most fluently. Unusually for an opening batsman, he was not a defensive player except in case of considerable need. His assault on Laker at Leeds in 1948 put that bowler out of the England side for two years. Surprisingly, for a left-hander he was murderously hard on right-arm off spinners.' There is more, which space considerations preclude, but John Arlott's final estimate must be quoted: 'A kindly, immensely likeable, honest man, he saw many friends when he came to England this summer (1983) and all of them must have hoped he will repeat the visit. Men as good as this are rare.' None would argue with this assessment.

To conclude this chapter, Alec Bedser and Arthur Morris, as noted, are very close friends and Bedser did much to negate the proposition that Morris was his 'bunny'. Writing of his friendly enemy's attitude to cricket in his book *Cricket Choice*, Bedser concludes with the following testimonial:

> Winning or losing Arthur was always the same cheerful spirit and a wide grin or chuckle was not far away in the sternest moments. His attitude was typified in a little incident at Sydney in 1950. Playing for an Australian XI against MCC, he had reached his century when he turned to me at the end of an over and said: 'Bob Berry hasn't got a wicket, and John Warr hasn't taken a catch all tour so I'll see what can be done.' Sure enough the scoreline reads: 'A R Morris c Warr b Berry 100.'
>
> I suppose in an age of pressure cricket and a fierce spotlight on every captain, Arthur was too nice a man to have the captaincy. But his impact was no less important. Eminent Australians with long memories earnestly compared the merits of Morris with legendary left-handers Clem Hill and Warren Bardsley, as later they did with Harvey. Not having had the privilege of seeing Hill or Bardsley, (though history and my informant Jack Hobbs vouched for their high ability), I am not in a position to judge where Morris stands. But even to be linked with two major players was compliment enough. If Hill and Bardsley were better than Morris or Harvey, the margin must have been so insignificant as not to count.

Again

Mainly

of Left-handers

Arthur reflects

ARTHUR MORRIS, NOW 72 YEARS OLD, leads a far from sedentary life. Living in Cessnock, he plays tennis regularly, arranging matters to match his more mature years. Time has taught him where to serve, or return service, so that in most cases the receiver has little option other than to return the ball somewhere sufficiently adjacent that Arthur rarely needs to 'bust a gut' to lay racquet on it. Timing is no problem—he has it at 72 as he did at 17.

Cessnock, a mining town, has a fair bit going for it. It lies in the Hunter River Valley, one of the State's most fertile areas, famous for its wine grapes, dairying and mixed farming pursuits and is conveniently placed close to the port of Newcastle. Arthur and Judith live a fairly relaxed life in the town, with monthly forays to Sydney for meetings as a director of the Trust Company of Australia. His mother lived in Sydney until her death early in 1992.

Judith, a Western Australian, whom he married in 1968, complements him perfectly. She is of Scottish descent and the pair met at a mutual friend's home.

In a lifetime which took in a lot of playing in many countries, Arthur Morris has met people from a wide selection of vocations. If cricketers predominate they by no means monopolise the gathering, although its fair to say that most were encountered through Arthur's engagement in cricket. Belted earls and dukes, royalty, a cross-section of politicians, civic dignitaries, prime ministers, writers, actors, all find a place at some time.

It is interesting that among politicians one who stands out in Arthur's memory is the late Arthur Augustus Calwell. It was Calwell's misfortune that his political fortunes suffered because of the twenty-year split in his party caused by his predecessor, as well as the fact that he was outshone in parliament and the country by the formidable talents and presence of R G Menzies. Calwell and Menzies were good friends despite political differences. The style of Menzies, his powerful and lucid advocacy of any sort of issue, his razor-sharp political brain and the massive dignity of his bearing dwarfed all contemporaries. Yet Arthur Morris recalls Arthur Calwell as a charming man and entertaining companion. Lacking all Menzies' surface qualities he perhaps reflected a generous and caring spirit lacking in his famous contemporary. Arthur Morris draws the comparison between Calwell and a man of today with less apparent but enduring gifts—John Howard. Both have suffered at the hands of colleagues, both been hounded and mocked by the media and both have been denied the top political job.

Arthur enjoyed playing with Stan McCabe and speaks of him enthusiastically. His early days in first-class cricket were played under the guidance of such luminaries as Stan McCabe and Bill O'Reilly. Their influence on what was, in any event, a likeable and modest personality was considerable. Bertie Oldfield was also still around although nearing the end of his career. Arthur was a fast learner.

He batted frequently against O'Reilly in the nets but did not really experience the tensions faced by batsmen when facing the 'Tiger' in the middle. There was no challenge for Bill at net practice and he contented himself by putting his arm over as required and issuing advice to team mates.

Sid Barnes bluntly rebuked Arthur after his initial first-class century, for lashing out at balls wide of the off stump. This admonition resulted in the elimination of the late cut from his repertoire. This is a pity—the stroke, once the hallmark of great batsmen from Trumper on, is now rarely seen in any sort of cricket. 'Not a business stroke' they say in Yorkshire—but in Yorkshire, most spectacular strokes fall into the non-business category!

Sid Barnes was a character. In his day, his occasional departures from the norms of on and off field behaviour eventually led to the premature end of his cricketing career. Today they'd go unnoticed. Nobody ever heard of Barnes disputing a decision or threatening umpires, knocking stumps over as he departed, all delightfully chivalrous aspects of today's game. Once, at Lord's, of all places, Sid added a fresh dimension to the light appeal—this request was usually made decorously, in hushed and pleading tones. Not so Sid Barnes. Jack Fingleton reported that in 1948, in Stygian gloom, Sid strode up the pitch to Umpire Chester and uttered in a tone midway between a request and a demand, the immortal words: 'Eh! the light.'

Arthur recalls rooming with Barnes in Brisbane where the first Test in 1946–47 was being played. Arthur was dismissed cheaply, Barnes got a few more than Arthur but both were feeling rather flat at the day's end, after watching Bradman and Hassett systematically demolishing the England attack. Sid said to Arthur, 'We'll just go back to our room, lock the door and sulk.' They didn't, but it lifted Arthur's spirits.

Arthur Morris played quite a lot of top class cricket with one who is generally regarded as the greatest player of all. Whether or not one enjoyed a close rapport with the man, and there are some of both persuasions, there is no argument about his extraordinary ability as batsman, captain and administrator. Arthur Morris is an unashamed Bradman supporter. From his first contact with Don as a child in Dungog in the late 1920s, he has admired him both as a cricketer and as a man. He found it an 'unbelievable experience to be invited to play in a Test match for Australia in 1946 under Bradman's captaincy'. Arthur found Bradman 'loyal to his team mates, enthusiastic both for their personal success and the team's success'. Morris says Bradman was always accessible for advice. 'He could be humble in respect of his own achievements and, once you were accepted as a friend, a delightful and interesting companion' concludes Arthur, adding praise for Bradman's contribution to cricket on and off the field.

Of all his opening partners, Morris found Barnes the most effective. Bill Brown, Jim Burke, Colin McDonald, Jack Moroney and Les Favell all shared the top spot over the Morris years. Brown and Barnes stood out. They were always on the look-out for the quick single. The others mentioned needed a bit of prodding. It's interesting that Keith Miller, himself no dawdler, considered Morris the best runner he batted with.

In another Barnes story, Bill Hunt, the much loved Balmain left-hand bowler, figures. In a club match, Hunt was bowling to Barnes until, to his surprise, Sid stepped away from the wicket, held up his hand, and called down the pitch to the umpire, 'Stop him, umpire.' Not unreasonably the umpire asked the reason. Barnes: 'Tell him to put his cap on. The sun's glare from his bald head is distracting me.'

It has been often suggested that, in the 1946 Sydney Test, when Barnes and Bradman were both dismissed for 234 (Bradman departing first), Sid deliberately sacrificed his wicket so as not to upstage or outscore his captain. Arthur Morris thinks this unlikely. Among Sid's many laudable qualities, chivalry was not conspicuous in circumstances such as this. Indeed, Morris thinks it extremely unlikely that Barnes ever gave his wicket away in any sort of cricket, let alone when batting with Bradman. For all that, Sid and the Don seem to have hit it off very well, without being close friends. Bradman: reserved, controlled, precise; Barnes: abrasive, blunt, unconventional. They're an unlikely twosome whose one common trait was an insatiable appetite for runs. Both scored plenty.

With Bill O'Reilly and Lindsay Hassett as colleagues in 1956, a pair who at times displayed some unorthodox behaviour patterns, Arthur had some hair-raising drives around England. O'Reilly's navigation was apt to be up to 180° out resulting in some late arrivals at grounds where they were to report play. Morris recalls one particularly nervewracking journey from Ashby-de-la-Zouche in the South West to Manchester. The course appeared long and circuitous enough to have circled the United Kingdom before they landed, a little shaken up, at the Old Trafford ground.

The three were invited to visit Denis Compton in his attractive cottage on the Sunday of a match at the Oval. Denis had recently married for the third time and the trio were invited down to share an hospitable Sabbath with the newlyweds. The three, somewhat assorted as to size, duly arrived and were greeted enthusiastically by Denis who lost no time in producing his new partner. The lady was pleased to see the Australians but her greeting was a little limited by the presence of two very small dogs which she was carrying in her arms. The dogs were of the variety which make a noise far out of proportion to their size and they set up a noisy yapping in protest at the disturbance to their morning snooze. Mrs Compton soothingly explained to the dogs that these three gentlemen 'had come especially all the way from Australia' to see the mutts. Bill, ever gallant, and on his best behaviour, extended a friendly hand to pat one of them. It bit him. There followed a fair degree of consternation. Putting the culprit down, Mrs C. dashed off for the Band-aids, Denis for some antiseptic. Bill, his colour rising upwards from the neck in a manner familiar to a hundred or two batsmen around the globe who'd misguidedly hit him for four, picked up the offending animal and, with the timing and accuracy of a rugby five-eighth attempting a field goal, drop-kicked it into the wall opposite where it fell to the floor in stunned disbelief. From there it crawled back dejectedly towards Bill and, when the Comptons returned, was sitting at his feet, gazing upwards with an expression of mingled awe, disbelief and regret. Mrs Compton dressed Bill's finger remarking that the dog was making an attempt to apologise. Bill didn't feel the need either to add to or contradict this observation and the two spectators, with difficulty, maintained straight faces.

All the 1948 Australians were, says Arthur, back-foot players, as were Ponsford and McCabe. That is to say that if they came forward, they considered the ball to be of sufficiently full length to drive. The great majority of our best players have adhered to this general rule. So it's strange that in England where the proposition was first put by MacLaren, Grace and C B Fry 'play back or drive', we see now a predominace of batsmen eager at all costs to get on to the front foot to any delivery pitched on their own side of the wicket. During our period in the doldrums, in the late 70s and early 80s, the disease had spread here and was largely responsible for our troubles. It's still on view occasionally. In 1953 in England, many English players were caught comfortably in slips by the semi-umbrella fields set by Hassett and Morris. By 1956, when we suffered some of our worst defeats, most Australians were infected, and Laker and Lock had a bonanza.

Of the English fast bowlers on view during his time, Arthur thought Statham the best. Not as spectacular as Trueman or Tyson, and usually required to bowl upwind, his control and direction rarely strayed and he moved the ball both ways in the air and off the wicket. Tyson was the fastest of the three, Trueman master of the late outswinger at lively pace but Statham the most consistently reliable and hostile.

Richie Benaud recalls an authentic story relating to Arthur Morris and Lindsay Hassett. In 1959, Morris and Hassett were asked to play in the Prime Minister's Eleven against the visiting Englishmen. Arthur had recently splurged on a new bat and was playing a bit of district cricket. He was getting plenty of runs with it playing for Paddington to whom he'd transferred from St George. Arthur opened for the PM's XI and got 79 in his best style using the new bat. He hit Ted Dexter (England captain that year) for four fours in one over and heard Dexter say to Colin Cowdrey: 'Who is this old bastard?'

Lindsay Hassett followed Morris and asked if anyone would lend him a bat. Ever generous and on a high from his innings, Arthur offered Lindsay his bat. Hassett didn't get too many and, with Arthur and Richie watching in the company of Sir Robert Menzies, he was soon on his way back to the pavilion. While talking to Richie, Arthur overheard Sir Robert remark, 'How typical of Hassett, what a charming gesture— he really is the most wonderful man' Arthur turned to the PM and asked, 'What happened sir?' Menzies replied: 'Lindsay, as generous as ever, has given his bat to a little boy in the crowd.' 'His bat!' Morris yelled, throwing protocol to the wind, 'Pig's arse, it was my bloody bat.' To crown the incident, the youthful beneficiary later came to the dressing room and obtained all the players' signatures on the bat. Hassett, after signing his name said, with a mischievous glance towards Morris, 'And Mr Morris would certainly love to sign it for you.'

Quite recently, in April 1992, Arthur was honoured by having an oval in the Hunter Valley District at Pokolbin named after him. The ground, within the environs of the Kirkton Park Country Hotel, is larger than the Sydney Cricket Ground and the naming ceremony was carried out during an interval in a match between Hunter Valley lawyers and vignerons, with proceeds to go to the Hunter Mission and Sydney City Mission. The *Newcastle Herald* gave a fairly comprehensive review of Arthur Morris's life and career and noted that he'd captained Australia twice and been vice-captain in 25 Tests.

To return to the subject broached in my first chapter: where does Arthur stand in relation to the great left-handers of the past 60 years? I've been lucky enough to see all of them bat, withal in a sadly limited way in the case of some. The best of them, I believe, are Pollock, Sobers, Harvey, Morris and Woolley, not necessarily in that order. It would be difficult to differentiate between these. They are clearly ahead of the 'second division' which might comprise Border, Lawry, John Edrich, Leyland, Gower, Paynter and Taylor. On the bowling side one thinks of Voce, Johnston, Davidson, Verity, Underwood, Ironmonger, Reid, Fleetwood-Smith.

Although impractical, it's fun to pick an Eleven made up solely of left-handers. How does this collection shape up, in batting order?

MORRIS
EDRICH J
POLLOCK
HARVEY
WOOLLEY
SOBERS
DAVIDSON
MARSH
VERITY
VOCE
JOHNSTON

It has batting down to No 9—Verity has opened for England, three fastish bowlers, a classy left-hand orthodox leg spinner, with the incomparable Sobers to bowl in whatever style his captain requires. Woolley too, with 2068 first-class wickets at 19.8, would make this side virtually unbeatable.

From an Australian point of view solely, a pretty good combination can be produced:

MORRIS
LAWRY
HARVEY
BORDER
COWPER
MACKAY
DAVIDSON
MARSH
JOHNSTON
FLEETWOOD–SMITH
IRONMONGER

This side has a longish tail in Messrs Fleetwood-Smith, Johnston and Ironmonger, and some would present fielding problems to their captain. But it's still a fairly strong side, although many would cavil at the omission of Mark Taylor and Bruce Reid. The latter's fitness problems keep him out and Taylor, despite his fine batting in England against weak opponents in 1989, has a little way to go in establishing consistency. Lawry, not the most attractive of players, can't be accused of inconsistency and his wicket was never surrendered weakly.

Picking imaginary sides is a fairly futile exercise, but fascinating. How would that Australian Eleven fare against these from England?

EDRICH J
MEAD
LEYLAND
WOOLLEY
GOWER
PAYNTER
EVANS
VERITY

WARDLE OR LOCK

VOCE

LEVER J

There is no English wicket-keeper (hence Evans) nor fast left-hander of top quality to share the new ball with Voce. Lever's career was fairly brief but he was decidedly sharp and appears to be the best available. Otherwise the teams are fairly matched except that there is no England left-hand all-rounder of Davidson's quality. Woolley has legitimate all-round claims but bowled more in the fashion of Verity than as an opening bowler.

To wind up this exercise, I asked Arthur Morris to name his best Eleven from all countries playing as at July 1992. These are the people he chose in batting order:

TAYLOR	AUST
GOOCH	ENG. CAPTAIN
BOON	AUST
RICHARDSON	WEST INDIES
WAUGH M	AUST
BORDER	AUST
STEWART	ENG—WICKET-KEEPER
AMBROSE	WEST INDIES
AKRAM	PAKISTAN
McDERMOTT	AUST
MUSHTAQ AHMED	PAKISTAN

This team contains five Australians which appears generous, particularly, at this stage of his career, as regards Alan Border. Arthur omitted Tendulkar on the score of youth and cited the case of Ian Craig who suffered from extravagant expectations. Neil Harvey and Archie Jackson weren't much older when they made their maiden appearances and the little Indian's class is obvious from the first time he puts bat to ball. Apart from those niggles, Arthur's side would take some beating. What a pity we couldn't turn the clock back and match them with the giants of the past.

Postscript

NOW, IN MID-1994, Arthur is still living in Cessnock. He regularly plays tennis, usually dictating the play so that the need to run excessively is largely eliminated. He has some honorary jobs, including the 'Patronage' of the Narara-Wyoming Cricket Club and makes occasional speeches in a fluent, whimsical and self-effacing fashion in keeping with his personality. He maintains close relationships with Sir Ronald Brierley and Basil Sellers, who have contributed greatly to the game. He has a well-earned position in the Sport Australia Hall of Fame.

Bill O'Reilly and Lindsay Hassett, dear friends in cricket and beyond, both quit the scene in the past two years or so. Arthur mourned their passing and maintains contact with both Molly O'Reilly and Tess Hassett. Keith Miller, Bill Brown, Ian Johnson, Richie Benaud, Neil Harvey, Ken Archer and Bill Johnston are regular contacts either by letter or telephone.

Mark Taylor, who looked likely to parallel Arthur's achievements a few years ago but hasn't quite done so, has donned the mantle of Australian captain, and Arthur thinks he will serve Australia well. He has some fences to mend but could well have the character to do the repair work for the benefit of both players and the cricketing public.

Apart from growing a little older like the rest of us, Arthur is doing it gracefully while enjoying life. He takes one day at a time and is blessed with a caring and loving wife. Donald Trelford has written a book as recently as 1988 on the late Len Hutton. Arthur Morris is one who was asked to contribute some thoughts on the great batsman. He concluded his remarks with this sentence: 'He was always the gentleman and it was always a pleasure to see him.' Anyone who has known Arthur Morris would think the words apply equally to him. 'A man worth knowing' as the old Tiger would say.

Arthur Morris

b. Bondi, New South Wales, 19.1.1922

Season	M	Inn	NO	HS	Runs	Avrge	Ct	50
1940–41	4	7	—	148	386	55.14	2	—
1946–47	12	20	2	155	1234	68.55	5	5
1947–48	11	16	1	162	887	59.20	3	4
1948 Eng	21	29	2	290	1922	71.19	7	7
1948–49	9	17	1	177	1069	66.81	6	2
1949–50 S Af	18	27	3		1411	58.79	8	1
1950–51	15	22	1	206	1221	58.14	6	3
1951–52	8	13	—	253	698	53.69	2	—
1952–53	14	21	1	105	913	45.65	1	7
1953 Eng	25	37	3	126*	1302	38.29	1	11
1953–54	6	10	1	171	487	54.11	2	2
1954–55	8	12	—	153	382	31.83	1	1
1954–55 WI	7	11	—	157	577	52.45	2	2
1962–63 Ind/SAf	3	6	—	70	103	17.60	—	1
1963–64 Ind	1	2	—	20	22	11.00	—	—
	162	250	15	290	12614	53.67	46	46

Test Matches *(by rubber)*

1946–47 vs Eng	5	8	1	155	503	71.86	3	1
1947–48 vs Ind	4	5	1	100*	209	52.25	1	—
1948 vs Eng	5	9	1	196	696	87.00	3	3
1949–50 vs SAf	5	8	—	157	422	52.75	2	—
1950–51 vs Eng	5	9	—	206	321	35.67	1	1
1951–52 vs WI	4	8	—	48	186	23.25	—	—
1952–53 vsSAF	5	9	—	99	370	41.10	—	3
1953 vs Eng	5	10	—	89	337	33.70	—	3
1954–55 vs Eng	4	7	—	153	223	31.86	1	—
1954–55 vs WI	4	6	—	111	266	44.33	1	1
	46	79	3	206	3533	46.49	12	12

Test Matches *(by country)*

vs England	24	43	2	206	2080	50.73	8	8
vs S Africa	10	17	—	157	792	46.58	2	3
vs W Indies	8	14	—	111	452	33.00	1	1
vs India	4	5	1	100*	209	52.25	1	—
	46	79	3	206	3533	46.49	12	12

1940–41 in Australia   4–7–0*–386–55.14

NSW	v	Queensland (S)	c McCarthy b Cook	148	516
			c Tallon b Cook	111	9–369d
	v	Victoria (S)	c Meikle b Johnson	37	440
			b Sievers	1	175
	v	Victoria (M)	lbw b Ring	25	416
			c Baker b Sievers	31	304
	v	S Australia (A)	b Grimmett	33	512

1946–47 in Australia   12–20–2*–1234–68.55

NSW	v	Queensland (B)	run out	27	192
			lbw b Ellis	98	5–212
Aust XI	v	MCC (M)	c Evans b Yardley	115	5–327
NSW	v	MCC (S)	not out	81	4–165d
1st Test	v	England (B)	c Hammond b Bedser	2	645
2nd Test	v	England (S)	b Edrich	5	8–659d
NSW	v	Victoria (M)	c Miller b Freer	83	205

			c Johnson b Rigg	110	241
3rd Test	v	England (M)	lbw b Bedser	21	365
			b Bedser	155	536
NSW	v	Victoria (S)	c Baker b Tribe	37	329
			c Tribe b Freer	23	189
4th Test	v	England (A)	c Evans b. Bedser	122	487
			not out	124	1–215
NSW	v	S Australia (S)	c Dooland b O'Neill	13	145
			c Vaughton b Noblett	53	9–277d
NSW	v	MCC (S)	st Evans b Smith	44	342
			c Edrich b Pollard	47	6–262d
5th Test	v	England (S)	lbw b Bedser	57	253
			run out	17	5–214

1947–48 in Australia   11–16–1–*–887–59.20

NSW	v	Queensland (B)	c Archer b Ball	19	281
			c R Rogers b Carrigan	42	7–279d
	v	Indian XI (S)	c Ranvirsinhji		
			b Amir Elahi	162	8–561d
	v	Victoria (S)	c RN Harvey		
			b W Johnston	1	135
			c Ring b Jinks	31	246
1st Test	v	India (B)	hit wkt b Sarwate	47	8–382d
2nd Test	v	Australia (S)	lbw b Amarnath	10	107
NSW	v	S Australia (A)	lbw b Oswald	81	509
	v	Victoria (M)	c Freer b Ring	78	420
			c Johnson b Loxton	51	4–185
3rd Test	v	India (M)	b Amarnath	45	394
			not out	100	4–255d
NSW	v	S Australia (S)	c Langley b Dooland	78	374
			c Ridings b Jose	20	5–108d
4th Test	v	India (A)	b Phadkar	7	674
20th Aust	v	W Australia (P)	c (sub) Dick b Langdon	115	7–442d

1948 20th Australians in England 21–29–2*–1922–71.19

Aust XI	v	Worcestershire	c Jenkins b Jackson	138	8–462d
	v	Yorkshire	c and b Smailes	17	101
			c Hutton b Smailes	3	6–63
	v	Surrey	lbw b McMahon	65	632

		v	Cambridge Uni	c Pearson b Mills	26	4–414d
		v	Oxford Uni	run out	64	431
		v	MCC	lbw b Edrich	5	552
		v	Lancashire	c E Edrich b Pollard	22	204
				c G Edrich b Pollard	5	4–259
		v	Nottinghamshire	lbw b Jepson	16	400
		v	Sussex	c and b Langridge	184	5–549d
1st Test		v	England (TB)	b Laker	31	509
				b Bedser	9	2–98
		v	Northamptonsh	b Clarke	60	8–352d
2nd Test		v	England (L)	c Hutton b Coxon	105	350
				b Wright	62	7–460d
Aust XI		v	Gloucestershire	c and b Scott	290	7–774d
3rd Test		v	England (OT)	c Compton b Bedser	51	221
				not out	54	1–92
		v	Middlesex	c Brown b Young	108	317
4th Test		v	England (Lc)	c Cranston b Bedser	6	458
				c Pollard b Yardley	182	3–404
Aust XI		v	Warwickshire	hit wkt b Hollies	32	254
				not out	20	1–41
		v	Lancashire	c Wilson b Roberts	49	321
				c Place b Pollard	16	3–265d
5th Test		v	England (O)	run out	196	389
Aust XI		v	Kent	c Evans b Dovey	43	361
		v	Levenson-Gower	b Yardley	62	8–489d

1948–49 in Australia 9–17–1*–1069–66.81

NSW		v	Queensland (B)	c and b Mackay	120	499
				c Tallon b Swendsen	19	3–93
Bradman's		v	Hassett's XI (M)	c and b McCool	25	434
				c and b Barnes	108	9–402
NSW		v	W Australia (P)	b Langdon	163	507
		v	S Australia (A)	c Langley b Noblet	12	243
				b Noblet	61	4–353d
		v	Victoria (M)	hit wicket		
				b W Johnston	177	334
				b Lambert	39	6–200
		v	Queensland (S)	c Tallon b L Johnson	30	180
				not out	108	0–143
		v	Victoria (S)	c Hassett b Lambert	1	229

			c C McDonald		
			b Lambert	2	221
	v	S Australia (S)	lbw b McLean	110	261
			c Watts b Noblet	16	2–132
Morris	v	Hassett's XI (S)	c Miller b Ring	66	581
			c F Johnston b Walker	12	2–62

1949–50 Australians in South Africa 18–27–3*–1411–58.79

Aust XI	v	Natal	c Wade b McCarthy	10	275
			c Wade b McCarthy	153	2–280d
	v	NE Transvaal	c Miles b Waller	29	4–331d
			not out	13	0–19
	v	S Rhodesia	c Wallace b Mansell	104	398
	v	S African XI	c Begbie b Waddington	43	312
	v	Orange Free St	run out	33	3–405d
	v	W Province	c Reid b Bolus	3	235
			c Nel b Thwaites	22	6–216d
	v	Transvaal	c Mitchell b A Rowan	15	84
			lbw b Heaney	12	109
1st Test	v	Sth Africa (J)	c H Tayfield		
			b McCarthy	0	413
2nd Test	v	Sth Africa (CT)	c Watkins b H Tayfield	42	7–526d
			c and b Mann	24	2–87
Aust XI	v	Border	b Beesley	106	4–425d
3rd Test	v	Sth Africa (D)	c Smith b H Tayfield	25	75
			hit wkt b H Tayfield	44	5–336
Aust XI	v	Transvaal	c and b Begbie	103	223
			not out	35	3–61
	v	N E Transvaal	c Funston b Wiles	30	8–338d
4th Test	v	Sth Africa (J)	c Fullerton b McCarthy	111	8–465d
			c Mann b McCarthy	19	2–259
Aust XI	v	Griqualand West	c Henchie b McNally	50	9–355d
			not out	102	1–252d
5th Test	v	Sth Africa (PE)	c Winslow b Melle	157	7–549d
Aust XI	v	W Province	c Bolus b Thwaits	103	7–425d
	v	S African XI	c H Tayfield		
			b A Tayfield	23	227

1950–51 in Australia 15–22–1*–1221–58.14

NSW	v	Queensland (B)	c K Archer b Raymer	74	9–529d
	v	Queensland (S)	c Tallon b Smith	101	229
			not out	78	0–225
	v	MCC (S)	c Hutton b Bailey	168	3–509
	v	Victoria (M)	c and b Loxton	29	346
	v	S Australia (A)	c and b Noblet	26	484
1st Test	v	England (B)	lbw b Bedser	25	228
			c Bailey b Bedser	0	7–32
Aust XI	v	MCC (S)	c Warr b Bailey	100	9–526d
2nd Test	v	England (M)	c Hutton b Bedser	2	194
			lbw b Wright	18	181
NSW	v	MCC (S)	st Evans b Wright	105	333
			hit wkt b Brown	14	6–130
3rd Test	v	England (S)	b Bedser	0	426
Comb. Team	v	MCC (S)	c Compton b Bedser	7	289
			c Warr b Bedser	8	103
NSW	v	Victoria (S)	b I Johnson	182	7–459d
4th Test	v	England (A)	b Tattersall	206	371
			run out	16	8–403d
NSW	v	S Australia (S)	run out	8	398
5th Test	v	England (M)	lbw b Brown	50	217
			lbw b Bedser	4	197

1951–52 in Australia 8–13–8*–698–53.69

NSW	v	Queensland (B)	c K Archer b Raymer	253	400
1st Test	v	West Indies (B)	c Rae b Valentine	33	226
			c Gomez b Ramadhin	48	7–236
NSW	v	West Indians (S)	c Worrell b Gomez	4	239
2nd Test	v	West Indies (S)	cWalcott b Jones	11	517
			st Walcott b Ramadhin	30	3–137
NSW	v	Victoria (M)	c I McDonald b W Johnston	210	533
	v	Victoria (S)	c I McDonald b W Johnston	18	449
			c I McDonald b W Johnston	27	7–166

3rd Test	v	West Indies (A)	b Worrell	1	82
			b Valentine	45	255
4th Test	v	West Indies (M)	b Trim	6	216
			lbw b Valentine	12	9–260

1952–53 in Australia 14–21–1*–913–45.65

NSW	v	Queensland (B)	c Mackay b Raymer	95	499
	v	Queensland (S)	c Mackay b McCool	58	260
	v	S Africans (S)	c McLean b H Tayfield	55	289
			c Murray b H Tayfield	39	5–276
	v	Victoria (M)	c Hill b W Johnston	69	567
	v	S Australia (A)	c Hole b Manning	10	148
			b Manning	15	272
1st Test	v	Sth Africa (B)	lbw b Watkins	29	280
			c Melle b H Tayfield	58	277
2nd Test	v	Sth Africa (M)	c and b H Tayfield	43	243
			c Watkins b Melle	1	290
NSW		S Africans (S)	c Waite b Murray	12	7–416d
3rd Test	v	Sth Africa (S)	b Watkins	18	443
4th Test	v	Sth Africa (A)	c Endean b Fuller	1	530
			c Endean b Melle	77	3–233d
5th Test	v	Sth Africa (M)	run out	99	520
			lbw b H Tayfield	44	209
21st Aust	v	Tasmania (H)	lbw b Cowley	40	510
	v	Combined XI (L)	b Hird	34	469
			not out	11	0–41
	v	W Australia (P)	c Langdon b Outride	105	4–356d

1953 21st Australians in England 25–37–3*–1302–38.29

Aust XI	v	Worcester	c Richardson b Whitehead	17	7–452
	v	Yorkshire	b Burgin	57	6–453d
	v	Surrey	b Bedser	20	256
	v	Cambridge Uni	b Marlar	79	383
	v	MCC	c Sheppard b Moss	6	179
			not out	4	2–13
	v	Oxford Uni	c Jowett b Fasken	15	330
	v	Lancashire	b Marner	29	298
	v	Nottinghamshire	c Meads b Jepson	15	6–290

	v	Hampshire	c Walker b Cannings	55	268
			b Gray	50	5–169d
1st Test	v	England (TB)	lbw b Bedser	67	249
			b Tattersall	60	123
Aust XI	v	Derbyshire	lbw b Jackson	13	197
			c Dawkes b Gladwin	6	145
2nd Test	v	England (L)	st Evans b Bedser	30	346
			c Statham b Compton	89	368
Aust XI	v	Gloucestershire	c Emmett b Cook	26	9–402d
			not out	7	1–33
	v	Northamptonsh	c Brown b Tribe	80	323
3rd Test	v	England (OT)	b Bedser	1	318
			c Hutton b Laker	0	8–35
4th Test	v	England (Ld)	cLock b Bedser	10	266
			st Evans b Laker	38	4–147
Aust XI	v	Surrey	c Loader b Surridge	67	9–327
	v	Glamorgan	lbw b McConnon	48	386
	v	Lancashire	lbw b Tattersall	64	372
			c Grieves b Tattersall	38	3–106
	v	Essex	c Vigar b Preston	33	7–477d
5th Test	v	England (O)	lbw b Bedser	16	275
			lbw b Lock	26	162
Aust XI	v	Gentlemen/Eng	c May b Chesterton	12	154
			not out	126	2–253
	v	Kent	c Dovey b Shirreff	8	8–465d
	v	Comb. Services	b Spencer	0	4–592
	v	England XI	b Tattersall	20	317
			b Tattersall	70	8–325

1953–54 in Australia 6–10–1*–487–54.11

NSW	v	Queensland (B)	c and b Flynn	171	422
	v	S Australia (A)	c Ridings b Wilson	126	482
			c Stevens b Drennan	9	2–164
	v	Victoria (M)	lbw b Hill	70	461
			not out	27	1–71
	v	Queensland (S)	c Grout b R Archer	19	323
Morris' XI	v	Hassett's XI (M)	b Miller	7	562
			c Harvey b I Johnson	52	399

200

	v	Victoria (S)	c Maddocks b W Johnston	5	182
			c Power b W Johnston	1	319

1954–55 in Australia 8–12–0*–382–31.83

NSW	v	Queensland (B)	c Grout b Lindwall	27	9–469
	v	MCC (S)	c R T Simpson b Bedser	26	382
1st Test	v	England (B)	c Cowdrey b Bailey	153	8–601d
2nd Test	v	England (S)	c Hutton b Bailey	12	228
			lbw b Statham	10	184
NSW	v	Victoria (M)	lbw b Hill	28	206
			c Hill b Loxton	78	363
3rd Test	v	England (M)	lbw b Tyson	3	231
			c Cowdrey b Tyson	4	111
NSW	v	Victoria (S)	c Dick b Power	0	234
4th Test	v	England (A)	c Evans b Tyson	25	323
			c and b Appleyard	16	111

1954–55 Australians in the West Indies 7–11–0*–577–52.45

Aust XI	v	Jamaica	c Rae b Smith	157	453
			c Binns b Holt	22	9–319
1st Test	v	West Indies (K)	lbw b Valentine	65	9–515d
			c Gibbs b Weekes	1	1–20
Aust IX	v	Trinidad	run out	21	299
2nd Test	v	West Indies (T)	c King b Butler	111	9–600d
3rd Test	v	West Indies (G)	c Sobers b D Atkinson	44	257
			c Walcott b Marshall	38	2–133
Aust XI	v	Barbados	b D Atkinson	33	333
			lbw b Goddard	78	7–204
5th Testa	v	West Indies (K)	lbw b Dewdney	7	8–758d

1962–63 Cavaliers in India and South Africa 3–6–0*–103–17.16

Cavaliers	v	C Club of India	b Gupte	4	286
			lbw b Shivalkar	70	4–159d
	v	Transvaal	c Waite b Walker	14	272
			c Ritchie b Walker	0	334
	v	W Province	C Ferrandi b Partridge	7	255
			c Bromfield b Partridge	8	212

1963–64 in India 1–2–0*–22–11.00

President's		Prime Minister's	c Titmus		
XI	vs	XI————————	b Jaisimha———————	2	8–355d
			c Hunte b Wilson———	20	356

Index

ACKNOWLEDGMENTS

I am grateful to the following gentlemen for their recollections of Arthur Morris: Messrs Alec Bedser, Ian Johnson, Bill Johnston, Frank Tyson, Warren Saunders, Bill Brown, Ian Craig, Richie Benaud, Sam Loxton, Keith Miller, Bill O'Reilly (deceased 6 October 1992), Lindsay Hassett (deceased 16 June 1993), John 'Chappie' Dwyer (deceased 7 July 1994).

And many thanks to the following people or organisations who contributed in other ways: Ian McNamara (Australian Broadcasting Corporation), Dr Gerard Henderson (Executive Director of the Sydney Institute), Dr Colin Clowes (compiler of the statistical appendix) and New South Wales Cricket Association for access to the Association Library.

Special thanks to Jon Cleary, the noted Australian author, for his graceful foreword which summarises Arthur Morris's character in a memorable way.

All photographs are from Arthur Morris's private collection except Maurice Tate is courtesy of Ralph Barker's book *Ten Great Bowlers* and Alec Bedser is courtesy of Film World, Jack Egan and ABC Books' *The Bradman Era*.